Prayers of the Bible

Prayers of the Bible

EQUIPPING WOMEN TO CALL ON GOD IN TRUTH

Leader's Guide

SUSAN HUNT

P&R
PUBLISHING
P.O. BOX 817 • PHILLIPSBURG • NEW JERSEY 08865-0817

P&R Publishing permits the reproduction of individual handouts, in print form with appropriate credit, for noncommercial use. For any other use or quotation, please contact the publisher.

Printed in the United States of America

ISBN: 978-1-59638-388-3

CONTENTS

PREFACE

Dear Discipler of Women,

"I thank my God in all my remembrance of you . . . because of your partnership in the gospel" (Phil. 1:3–4).

I am grateful that God has called you to disciple His daughters. As I state in the text, I am committed to Titus 2 discipleship. T2D is life-on-life discipleship. It is a nurturing, mothering ministry. Paul captured the idea in his first letter to the Thessalonians.

> We were gentle among you, like a nursing mother taking care of her own children. So, being affectionately desirous of you, we were ready to share with you not only the gospel of God but also our own selves, because you had become very dear to us. (1 Thess. 2:7–8)

This Leader's Guide is designed to help you teach the gospel and encourage women to share life together. It includes more than lesson plans. There are also suggestions for building community among the women. This relational component is essential to cultivate a safe, loving context to study the Word and to pray together.

The lesson plans are not intended for a lecture format. These are interactive studies that help you expand and apply the material in the text.

My prayers are with you as you disciple women to be true women who call on God in truth.

For God's Glory,
Susan

INTRODUCTION

Preparing to Teach

The following suggestions should be adapted to your group, schedule, and style.

Using the Material

- Text (student book): Encourage women to read the text in advance.
- Reflect and Pray: Each chapter concludes with suggestions for reflection. Encourage the women to use notebooks to record their thoughts and prayers. Suggestion: Many women are in seasons of life where they feel overwhelmed. Emphasize that reading the material in advance is not a requirement.
- Lesson Plan: The lesson plans review, reinforce, and expand the material in the text.
- Handouts: The handouts at the end of each lesson plan in this Leader's Guide correlate with the lesson plan. Make copies and encourage the women to keep them in their notebooks, since you will frequently refer back to handouts from previous lessons.

Preparing the Lesson

- Read the Scripture and the text.
- Do the assignments in the Reflect and Pray section of the text.
- Read the Leader's Guide and handout.
- Prayerfully read the Scripture again several times.
- Pray for the women you teach as you plan your lesson.

Preparing for Prayer

- Pray for wisdom to help the women grow in their corporate prayer life. Do not just study about prayer. Be intentional in spending time learning to pray.
- Suggestions: Have several prayer times—a time of praise, another time to use a prayer sheet listing church needs, and a time when women can share their prayer requests and pray for one another. Encourage women to use their notebooks to record requests and the date. Later you can go back to these and record answers to prayer. The lesson plan sometimes suggests prayer times during the lesson.

Bible Study Committee

A committee involves more women in leadership and relieves the teacher of responsibilities other than preparing the lesson. You may ask women to assume responsibility for the following:

- Greeting: Welcome women and provide name tags.
- Refreshments: Organize volunteers to provide snacks.

- Prayer: Have a prayer sheet each week with church prayer requests. Also list a staff member, elder and deacon, and their families. List a missionary your church supports. These prayer sheets can also be kept in the notebooks.
- Building community: This is an essential element to give women an opportunity to share their joys and sorrows and to pray for one another. Women are unlikely to do this with strangers. Providing ways for women to build relationships will transform your Bible study from an academic atmosphere to a loving and safe place. Ideas for building community are listed below.

Suggested Class Format

- Gathering, refreshments
- Welcome and opening prayer
- Community building activity
- Lesson and prayer times

You may want to include singing. Idea: Sometimes use a hymn as a prayer.

Be flexible. If a woman arrives who is distraught because of a crisis in her life, forget your format and gather the women around her to pray for her.

Ideas for building community

This is an intentional way to help women build relationships. This segment should not be more than ten to fifteen minutes. Here are a few ideas:

- Ask someone who enjoys crafts to plan an activity for the women to make bookmarks with Psalm 145:18.
- Use the prayers at the end of the text to make prayer cards. These may be personalized, put on index or business-size cards, with holes punched in the corners and tied together with ribbon.
- Life-giving prayer stories: After the women have read two or three chapters, ask any who have or know similar stories to write them. Schedule volunteers to read their stories.
- Ask someone from the missions committee to have prayer cards of missionaries supported by the church. Distribute these and ask women to "introduce" the missionaries whose names they received. Ask them to follow up by praying for and corresponding with the missionaries and to give updates whenever they receive prayer requests from them.
- Do the same with the names of shut-ins, church staff, elders, deacons, Sunday school teachers, and others who serve in the church. Assign names to women and ask them to contact the persons and find out whether they have specific prayer requests.
- Sign cards of appreciation for families of church staff, elders and deacons, college students, etc. Have a time of prayer for those who will receive the cards.
- Box talks and testimonies are excellent ways for the women to know one another. Explanations and guidelines are below. When someone volunteers, give her a copy of the guidelines. Emphasize the time limit. These ideas can be used frequently.

Guidelines for Box Talks

What is a box talk? It is a "show and tell" for grown-ups. It is a delightful way to get to know one another.

What do you do? You place in a container (a box, bag, basket, etc.) objects that are representative of you and your life, and then you show the objects one at a time and tell why you included them. A box talk should be short and concise, giving a glimpse into who you are and what you love. It should be a catalyst for further conversations. The guidelines below are intended to help you prepare.

The purpose of box talks:

- To nurture community among the women in a group by helping them to know one another better.
- For the woman who is reporting to have the opportunity to learn to speak concisely, intentionally, and purposefully. This is an important aspect of our discipleship.

Guidelines to keep these talks interesting and lively:

- Choose five to seven items that represent who you are. Pray about these items and choose them carefully. Pray for wisdom to know which parts of your life will help you connect to the women in the group.
- Use items that tell something about yourself, and let the item do the talking. A couple of sentences of explanation are sufficient. Women can talk with you afterward about specific points of interest.
- Use pictures sparingly because it is difficult for everyone to see the picture and awkward to pass around too many pictures. Other items that make a box talk stronger include a favorite book, or something that depicts a hobby or vacation spot,

something that recalls a special moment or a future dream, or an item of clothing that recalls a special memory. For example, an old spoon that belonged to your grandmother who taught you to cook and to pray for the people who would sit at your table communicates a myriad of messages. Be prayerful and creative as you select items to show.

- Although your box talk is not a testimony, consider including a single aspect of your testimony or a specific spiritual lesson you learned from another person or an event in your life.
- Decide the best order to show the items and then list them in that order. Do not emphasize details (too much information is too much information!).
- **A box talk should not exceed five minutes.** It is important to plan carefully because it is easy to think you have talked for five minutes when it has actually been twenty-five minutes. PLEASE, do not mention time. References to "they only gave me five minutes," or "I think my time is up but . . ." take time and deflect from your box talk.

Guidelines for Testimonies

An essential part of discipleship is learning to give a testimony, and an essential part of community is sharing these stories of God's grace.

Guidelines to help you prepare:

- Time: 3 to 5 minutes

- Pray
  - That your words will point to Jesus and glorify Him.
  - That God, who knows your audience, will give you the words and love for the specific women who will hear.

- Gospel orientation
  - A testimony should focus on the gospel. It should include a clear statement of the gospel and the impact of the gospel in your life.
  - A testimony should not glorify sin by giving explicit details.

- Prepare
  - Write the testimony, then ask yourself these questions:
    (1) Will an unbeliever hear this and know how to become a Christian?
    (2) Is the testimony more about my feelings and experiences, or about God's Word and His work in my life?
    (3) Is the focus on Jesus or on myself?
  - Practice and edit the testimony until it is 30 seconds shorter than the time allotted. This will not detract from the message. A clear, focused testimony is much more effective than a rambling, repetitive one.
  - When you share a testimony, it is suggested that you read what you have prepared.
  - Do not refer to the time—"My time is up but . . ." takes time and distracts the hearers.

The LORD is near to all who call on him,

to all who call on him in truth.

Psalm 145:18

1

REDEEMED: LESSON PLAN

GENESIS 1–3

1. Refer to the Introduction in the text, and begin with a brief discussion about Titus 2 discipleship.
   - Do you think that women need opportunities to learn from other women? Why or why not?

The following excerpts from *Women's Ministry in the Local Church* may be helpful to expand this discussion.

> We ought to have an intentional, deliberate approach to female discipleship because men and women are different, and these differences need to be recognized, taken into account, and addressed in the course of Christian discipleship.[1]

1. J. Ligon Duncan and Susan Hunt, *Women's Ministry in the Local Church* (Wheaton, IL: Crossway Books, 2006), 115.

Biblical discipleship is not simply imparting facts or inculcating personal habits of Bible study, prayer, and evangelism, as helpful as those disciplines are. It is transmitting a way of thinking and living that unites all the parts into the glorious whole of glorifying God. It is passing on a legacy of biblical faith and life to the next generation.[2]

Godly women who have embraced the truth of God's creation design and redemptive calling for women are called to train other women to think and live according to biblical principles of womanhood. This is the kind of life-on-life discipleship that guides and nurtures to maturity.[3]

Titus 2 gives legitimacy and limitations to a women's ministry. There is an unmistakable mandate for women to train women, but the extent of this training is somewhat limited. There are many times and places in church life where men and women study and serve side by side, but a primary task of the women's ministry is to train women in the biblical principles and practices of womanhood. This does not mean that biblical womanhood is the only thing that women study, but it does mean that there should be a resolute commitment to weave these principles throughout the entire women's ministry.[4]

- Read 1 Thessalonians 2:7–8. Explain that the various elements planned for your time together (fellowship, community building, prayer as well as study) are intended to help you share the gospel as well as your lives with one another.

2. Ibid., 123.
3. Ibid., 124.
4. Ibid., 127.

2. The principles in chapter one lay the foundation for our study of prayer. Each prayer we will consider has its roots in truths we see in Ephesians 1 and Genesis 1–3.

3. Read the first paragraph in chapter one: "Biblical womanhood . . . amazing gospel story."
   - We must be careful not to take any topic and lift it from the context of the whole of Scripture. To do so minimizes the scope of a passage. Throughout this study we will look at passages in light of the redemption story.
   - Handout question 1: Read the quotation from Dr. Edmund Clowney.

4. Handout question 2: Before the Beginning
   - The Father chose us in Christ before creation.
   - The Son redeemed us through His blood.
   - The Spirit seals and guarantees our inheritance.
   - What is the triune God's purpose? To praise His glorious grace.
   - What is this agreement among the persons of the Trinity called? The covenant of redemption.

5. Text, Reflect and Pray question 1: Spend time thanking God for the splendor of salvation. Ask volunteers to read their prayers based on Ephesians 1:1–14. You may want to ask three or four women in advance to be prepared to do this.
   - Suggestion: Whenever you have times of praise, you may want to ask the women to say "Amen" together after each woman prays. It may feel awkward at first,

but explain that it is a helpful way to keep our minds and hearts engaged as others pray.

6. Handout question 3: What is a covenant?
   - Briefly discuss the idea of covenant by summarizing the quotations, or ask women to read them. Another option: Encourage women to read this on their own.

7. Handout question 4: The Beginning
   - What are the three foundational realities discussed in the chapter?
     (1) Our authority is God's Word.
     (2) Our purpose is God's glory.
     (3) Gender distinctiveness is God's plan.

   - Text, Reflect and Pray question 2: Discuss each of these questions.
     (1) How does this differ from the cultural perspective of authority? The world tells women that we are our own authority and that independence is power. Submitting to God's authority in every area of life is essential for growth in Christ. Prayer is an act of acknowledging God's sovereignty and submitting to His authority.
     (2) How does this differ from the cultural perspective of our life purpose? A young woman once asked me whether it wasn't egotistical of God to create us for His glory. This was an honest question by someone steeped in this world's perspective that we exist for our own pleasure. My answer: There is no other purpose that could give us true significance. We are created to live in personal relationship with the

> majestic King of kings. As we live face-to-face with Him, we begin to look more and more like Him. Any other purpose is pitiful compared with that.

Paul David Tripp writes:

> Perhaps you're thinking . . . "How does it help me to have God's zeal for his own glory be greater than his zeal for anything else?" This is a very good question. . . .
>
> If God were to deny his own glory, he would by that act cease to be God. To be God, he must be above and beyond every created thing. Willingness to subjugate himself to anything other than himself would cause him to no longer be Lord over all. God's zeal for his glory really is the hope of the universe. . . . God's unshakable commitment to his own glory is the most loving thing he could ever do for us. It's what redeems us from us and breaks our bondage to all the things in life that we wrongly think will give us life but lead only to emptiness and ultimately death.[5]

> (3) What is your reaction to the quotation from Wayne Grudem? Emphasize that the world minimizes gender distinctiveness and says equality means sameness. This is absurd. It minimizes the value of our femaleness but, far worse, it minimizes our capacity to glorify God.

You may want to clarify that biblical headship and submission have reference to the home and church, not the marketplace. Also, a woman is never to submit to sin. We are to obey God and not man. For example, a woman who submits to abuse, or

5. Paul David Tripp, *Whiter Than Snow* (Wheaton, IL: Crossway Books, 2008), 127.

who hides her husband's drug addiction, is not a true helper to her husband. His actions are not her fault, but her response is her responsibility.

- The Westminster Shorter Catechism succinctly summarizes the first two foundational realities. Refer to these on the handout. Read the questions and ask the women to read the answers.

8. God's Female Design
   - Briefly summarize this section and ask for reactions.

9. Sin
   - Summarize this section in the text and emphasize that apart from a relationship with Jesus we do not have the desire or ability to glorify Him.
   - Handout question 5: The True and the New—What's the Difference?

The True Woman's purpose is God's glory, and her authority is God's Word.

The New Woman's purpose is her happiness, and her authority is herself.

10. Redemption
    - Handout question 6: The gospel. Read Genesis 3:15. Emphasize that man did not seek God. God took the initiative in reestablishing this relationship. God said, "You can't, but I will." Ask the women to circle the

words "I will" and to write in the margin: sovereign initiative/sovereign grace.

- Ask volunteers to read the covenant promise verses and to notice how this promise runs throughout Scripture. Note that in most of the verses we read the words "I will"—it is always God's sovereign grace that reaches out to us. God bound Himself to us with this promise. The promise was kept when Jesus came (Matt. 1:23; John 1:14).
- Suggestion: Process the amazing grace of this promise by asking two or three women to lead in prayer, thanking God for keeping His promise.

We will see the significance of this covenant promise in the prayers we will study.

11. Handout question 7: Eve means life-giver.
    - Use the True Woman/New Woman chart to discuss the contrast. Also use Reflect and Pray question 3.
    - Since the true woman lives for God's glory, she will be a life-giver in her relationships and circumstances. The new woman lives for self, so she will be a life-taker.
    - Encourage women to think of specific applications of each helper description. Some examples:

      Women breathe life into the church when they support the decisions of elders. They drain life out of the church when they weaken the leadership by criticizing decisions.

A woman gives life to her marriage when she protects the reputation of her husband rather than complaining about him to her children and friends.

- Refer to the question about a difficult relationship and explain that it may not be appropriate to share this. Nothing should be shared that would expose the sin of another person.
- How were the women in the Life-giving Prayer story life-givers? They were "stalwart defenders" in prayer. Each of the helper words can be seen in the prayer life of a true woman.
- You will refer to the True Woman/New Woman chart throughout the study.

12. Read the true woman statement in the text.
    - Read the question "How Do We Call on God in Truth?" and the answer.

13. Ask whether there are comments or reactions to the material you have covered.

14. Conclude with a time of prayer. It is important for women to have a time to share their prayer requests. If your group is large, you may want to divide into smaller groups for this.

1

REDEEMED: HANDOUT

Genesis 1–3

1. Edmund P. Clowney wrote:

> "The Greatest Story Ever Told"—this title has been used for the Bible, and with good reason. The Bible is the greatest storybook, not just because it is full of wonderful stories but because it tells one *great* story, the story of Jesus. . . .
>
> Anyone who has had Bible stories read to him as a child knows that there are great stories in the Bible. But it is possible to know Bible stories, yet miss *the* Bible story. . . . The Bible has a story line. It traces an unfolding drama. . . . The story is God's story. It describes His work to rescue rebels from their folly, guilt, and ruin. And in His rescue operation, God always takes the initiative. . . .
>
> Only God's revelation could maintain a drama that stretches over thousands of years as though they were days or hours. Only God's revelation can build a story where the end is anticipated from the beginning, and where the guiding principle is not chance or fate, but promise.[1]

1. Edmund P. Clowney, *The Unfolding Mystery: Discovering Christ in the Old Testament* (Phillipsburg, NJ: P&R Publishing, 1988), 9–13.

2. Before the Beginning

   vv. 3–6: The Father ___________ us in __________ before creation.

   vv. 7–12: The Son _______________ us through His ____________.

   vv. 13–14: The Spirit seals and guarantees our __________________.

   vv. 6, 12, 14: What is the triune God's purpose? ______________.

   What is this agreement among the persons of the Trinity called? _________.

3. What is a covenant?

   O. Palmer Robertson:

   A covenant may be defined as a bond in blood sovereignly administered. Life and death are at stake in the divine covenants. God has bound himself to humans and them to himself.[2]

   Michael Horton:

   God's very existence is covenantal: Father, Son, and Holy Spirit live in unceasing devotion to each other, reaching outward beyond the Godhead to create a community of creatures serving as a giant analogy of the Godhead's relationship. Created in the image of the Triune God, we are by nature outgoing, interdependent relationship establishers, finding ourselves in the other and not just in ourselves. Unlike the persons of the Trinity, we at one time did not exist. But when God did decide

2. O. Palmer Robertson, *Covenants* (Norcross, GA: Great Commission Publications, 1993), 11.

to create, his decree was not that of a lonely monarch, but of a delighted Father, Son, and Holy Spirit establishing a creaturely, finite analogy of their eternal giving and receiving relationship. We were not just created and then *given* a covenant; we were created *as* covenant creatures—partners not in deity, to be sure, but in the drama that was about to unfold in history.[3]

4. The Beginning

   What are the three foundational realities mentioned in the book?

   (1) ________________________________

   (2) ________________________________

   (3) ________________________________

Westminster Shorter Catechism:

Q. 1. What is the chief end of man?
A. Man's chief end is to glorify God, and to enjoy him for ever.

Q. 2. What rule hath God given to direct us how we may glorify and enjoy him?
A. The Word of God, which is contained in the Scriptures of the Old and New Testaments, is the only rule to direct us how we may glorify and enjoy him.

5. The True and the New—What's the difference?

	The True Woman	***The New Woman***
Purpose:	______________	______________
Authority:	______________	______________

3. Michael Horton, *God of Promise* (Grand Rapids: Baker Books, 2006), 10.

6. The gospel: "I will put enmity between you and the woman, and between your offspring and her offspring; he shall bruise your head, and you shall bruise his heel" (Gen. 3:15).

   God's covenant promise is woven throughout Scripture:

Genesis 17:7	Ezekiel 36:25–28
Exodus 6:7	Zechariah 8:7–8
Leviticus 26:12	Matthew 1:23
Deuteronomy 29:10, 12–13	John 1:14
Jeremiah 24:7	2 Corinthians 6:16
Jeremiah 31:33 and Hebrews 8:10	Revelation 21:1–4

7. Eve means ______________________________

The True Woman *Helper/Life-giver*	*The New Woman* *Hinderer/Life-taker*
Exodus 18:4 Defends	Attacks
Psalm 10:14 Sees, cares for oppressed	Indifferent, unconcerned for oppressed
Psalm 20:2 Supports	Weakens
Psalm 33:20 Shields, protects	Leaves unprotected
Psalm 70:5 Delivers from distress	Causes distress
Psalm 72:12–14 Pities the poor, weak, needy	Ignores poor, weak, needy
Psalm 86:17 Comforts	Causes discomfort

The LORD is near to all who call on him,

to all who call on him in truth.

Psalm 145:18

2

GLORIFY: LESSON PLAN

John 17:1–5

Preparation Suggestion: Chapter one gives an overview of God's eternal plan and purpose. Because every prayer in this study has its roots in Ephesians 1 and Genesis 1–3, you are encouraged to scan chapter one as you prepare each lesson. Continually remind the women of the foundational concepts in these passages.

1. Review with questions such as:
   - What are the three foundational realities we saw in chapter one?
   - What is a true woman's authority? Purpose?
   - What is a new woman's authority? Purpose?
   - What is the covenant promise? (I will be your God, you will be my people, I will dwell among you.)
   - As you have reflected on the language of biblical womanhood—helper, life-giver—how is this shaping your thinking about womanhood?

- What is the first answer to the question How Do We Call on God in Truth? (With gratitude for our redemption.)
- Have a time of prayer and encourage women to express their gratitude to God.

2. Chapter two (in text): Read the first paragraph. Read the last sentence of the quotation from James Boice or share your own perspective on studying this prayer.

3. Handout question 1: Briefly review the Overview section of the text.

4. Text, Reflect and Pray questions 1 and 2: What preceded and followed this prayer?
   - Discuss the deep love of Jesus as He washed the disciples' feet. Ask whether any of His final teachings to the disciples had particular significance to any of the women.

5. Read John 16:33–17:1
   - Jesus had been saying His final words to His disciples, then He turned His eyes to His Father.
   - Refer to the text and read the quotation: "From preaching He passed to prayer. . . ."
   - Discuss the true woman statement with questions such as: What is your reaction to this statement? Are you often overwhelmed with your situation? What difference does it make when we shift our focus from the situation to our Heavenly Father?

Women who are in difficult situations they cannot alter should find comfort in this statement. For example, a woman with a rebellious adult child can do nothing to change that behavior. We do all we can for our children while they are in our care, but the time comes when there is nothing we can do except the most important thing—pray for them.

6. Read John 17:1–5
   - Handout question 2: Fill in the blanks and ask whether there are questions or comments.

7. Handout question 3
   - Fill in the blanks: redemption, authority, eternal life, those the Father had given Him.
   - Text: Read the paragraph, "As Jesus approached the cross He was consumed. . . ."
   - Text, Reflect and Pray question 3: How many times did Jesus refer to those the Father gave Him?
   - Ask for reactions to the amazing fact that we were on His heart and mind, and that we still are.

8. Read John 17:3
   - Handout question 4: Eternal life is knowing God by knowing Jesus.
   - Text, Reflect and Pray question 4: Ask volunteers to read their summaries of these passages. You may want to begin by asking various women to read the verses.
   - Handout question 4: Read the quotations from James Boice and J. I. Packer.
   - Handout question 4: Read the true woman statement and ask for reactions.

9. Read John 17:4
    - Discuss this section. Emphasize that our calling is to glorify God in specific relationships and situations and that He has sovereignly ordained them.
    - Ask: What difference would it make if I view my daily responsibilities and relationships as the platform for me to fulfill my calling to glorify God? What difference would it make if I view my situations—financial, health, life season—as opportunities to glorify God?
    - Text: Refer to the Life-giving Prayer story. What difference is it making for Joni Tada?
    - Emphasize that the difference may not be a change in the relationships and situations, but there will be a difference in us. We will know Christ better.

10. Handout question 5
    - In these opening verses of John 17 are four themes that we will see in other prayers we will study. As we see how these themes shape other prayers it will help us to better understand God's nearness and our privilege of calling on Him in truth. It will also help us see how these themes should shape our own prayers.
    - Various themes could be mentioned but the ones identified in the text, and that future lessons will reinforce, are:

      God's glory
      God's people (those the Father gave the Son)
      God's nearness (knowing God)
      God's calling (the work God gave us to do)

11. Handout question 6
    - Fill in the blanks: glory, plan, purpose.
    - What difference would it make if we pray for God's glory? Concern for His glory lifts our hearts from ourselves to our glorious God. We begin to focus on the grand and glorious purpose for which we were created. We begin to see that our situation is our opportunity to glorify Him. The true woman prays that God will show her how to glorify Him in her situation.
    - What is necessary for us to pray according to God's plan and purpose? We must know His Word. The more we understand the over-arching story of the Bible, the more we can pray according to His plan and purpose.
    - Read the quotation from John Calvin on the handout.
    - You may want to ask the women to write a brief "true woman statement" that incorporates these principles as well as the principle of approaching God with gratitude for our redemption. Ask volunteers to read their statements.

2

GLORIFY: HANDOUT

John 17:1–5

1. The prayer divides into three sections:
   vv. 1–5: Christ's prayer for ____________________
   vv. 6–19: His prayer for His ____________________
   vv. 20–26: His prayer for ____________________

2. vv. 1 and 5: The first petition
   In the first petition Jesus prays for Himself: that the Father would ______________ Jesus and that Jesus would ____________________ the Father.
   There are 2 aspects of God's glory:
   (1) ____
   (2) ____

3. v. 2: Reason for this petition
   ______________________________ hinged on this petition.
   The Father had given the Son universal ____________________ in order that the Son could give ____________________ to ____________________.

4. v. 3

   Jesus clearly and concisely explains that eternal life is

   ______________________.

James Boice wrote:

> Knowledge of God and of ourselves go together. . . . It is a personal encounter with God in which, because of his holiness, we become aware of our sin and consequently of our deep personal need and then, by his grace, are turned to Christ who is our Savior. This knowledge occurs only where God's Holy Spirit is at work beforehand to make it possible, and it always changes us, issuing in a heart response to God and true devotion.[1]

In his classic book, *Knowing God*, J. I. Packer wrote:

> What were we made for? To know God.
> What aim should we set ourselves in life? To know God.
> What is the "eternal life" that Jesus gives? Knowledge of God . . . (John 17:3).
> What is the best thing in life, bringing more joy, delight and contentment than anything else? Knowledge of God. (Jer. 9:23–24)[2]

The true woman knows that she knows God because He first knew her and gave her to Christ. His love compels her to study His Word to know Him more intimately and to obey Him more faithfully.

1. James Montgomery Boice, *The Gospel of John, Vol. 4, Peace in Storm* (Grand Rapids: Baker Books, 1985, 1999), 1259.

2. J. I. Packer, *Knowing God, 20th Anniversary Edition* (Downers Grove, IL: InterVarsity Press, 1993), 33.

5. There are four themes in John 17:1–5 that we will see in other prayers we study:
   (1)
   (2)
   (3)
   (4)

6. What principles of calling on God in truth do we see in John 17:1–5?
   Pray for His ___________________.
   Pray according to God's eternal _______________ and _________.

John Calvin wrote on this passage:

> Christ asks that his kingdom may be glorified, in order that he also may advance the glory of the Father. . . . It is also the object of Christ's prayer, that his death may produce, through the power of the Heavenly Spirit, such fruit as had been decreed by the eternal purpose of God.

Calvin continues by referring to the words *since you have given him*:

> He again confirms the statement, that he asks nothing but what is agreeable to the will of the Father; as it is a constant rule of prayer not to ask more than God would freely bestow; for nothing is more contrary to reason, than to bring forward in the presence of God whatever we choose.[3]

3. John Calvin, *Calvin's Commentaries, John's Gospel—Vol. II* (Grand Rapids: Wm. B. Eerdmans Publishing, 1956), 164–65.

The LORD is near to all who call on him,

to all who call on him in truth.

Psalm 145:18

3

SANCTIFY: LESSON PLAN

John 17:6–19

1. Briefly review with questions such as:
   - What are the three divisions of this prayer? Christ's prayer for Himself, for His disciples, and for those who would follow.
   - Jesus' first petition is that God will glorify Him that He might glorify the Father. What hinges on this petition? Redemption.
   - What are the two aspects of God's glory? Internal (His attributes) and external (visible manifestations of brilliant light).
   - What are the four themes we see in John 17:1–5? God's glory, God's people, God's nearness, God's calling. Encourage the women to look for these themes in the remainder of this prayer and emphasize that we will see them in other prayers we will study.
   - As you reflect on chapters one and two, how are they shaping your thoughts about womanhood and about prayer?

2. Read John 17:6–19
   - Reflect and Pray question 1: Ask two or three volunteers to read their prayers based on this passage. You may want to ask them in advance, and then ask if there are other volunteers.

3. There are two petitions in this section. Although He makes reference specifically to the disciples, these two petitions, as well as the two in the next section, refer to the disciples and those who will follow them. They refer to all those the Father gave to Jesus.

4. Read verse 6
   - Handout question 1: Jesus tells us four things about those for whom He prays:
     (1) They are God's: God owns everything by right of creation. This refers to possession by redemption.
     (2) God gave them to Jesus.

Ask a volunteer to read the quotation from John Calvin.

(3) Jesus made God's name known to them. Note: Some translations say, "I have revealed you," but the literal translation is "revealed your name." What is the name of God that Jesus revealed in a unique way? Father.

Refer to the handout and ask whether anyone can think of the exception. Ask a volunteer to read Matthew 27:45–46. The following quotations will help you explain and expand on this. Emphasize that Jesus was forsaken by God so that those the Father gave Him never will be. His forsakenness was the price of our nearness.

James Boice writes:

Not only do all four Gospels record that Jesus used this address, they also report that he did so in all his prayers. . . . The only exception is one that actually enforces the importance of this title. It is the cry from the cross ("My God, my God, why have you forsaken me?") pronounced at that moment in which Jesus was made sin for us and the fellowship which he had enjoyed with the Father previously was temporarily broken.[1]

The *ESV Study Bible* notes explain:

Jesus quotes Ps. 22:1 . . . **My God, my God, why have you forsaken me?** Some of the most profoundly mysterious words in the entire Bible. In some sense Jesus had to be cut off from the favor of and fellowship with the Father that had been his eternally, because he was bearing the sins of his people and therefore enduring God's wrath . . . and yet, in quoting Ps. 22:1, Jesus probably has in mind the remainder of the psalm as well, which moves on to a cry of victory (Ps. 22:21–31); and he expresses faith, calling God "my God." Surely he knows why he is dying, for this was the purpose of his coming to earth. . . . And surely his cry, uttered **with a loud voice**, is expressing, not bewilderment at his plight, but witness to the bystanders, and through them to the world, that he was experiencing God-forsakenness not for anything in himself but for the salvation of others. Surely Matthew, understanding this, quotes Jesus' words to challenge his readers. Jesus' torment, despite his anticipations of it in Gethsemane, was surely inconceivable in advance.[2]

1. Boice, *The Gospel of John, Vol. 4, Peace in Storm,* 1273.

2. *English Standard Version Study Bible* (Wheaton, IL: Crossway Bibles, 2008), 1886.

Read the verses on the handout where Jesus addresses God as Father.

Reflect and Pray question 2: What are your thoughts about the privilege of calling the King of kings "Father"?

(4) They kept God's word

Summarize these thoughts from James Boice:

> Who were they, these few disciples? They understood little of his teaching . . . they obviously failed to understand the meaning and necessity of his death. . . . Weakness? Poverty of understanding? Yes, but there was strength too. It was not their own. It was only the result of the word of Christ that had by now entered into them. But the words *were* within them. That is the point. Like a seed planted in fruitful ground, those words would sprout into the fullness of a fruitful spiritual life. They were alive—that is what we really want to say—spiritually alive. Therefore the Lord could be confident, saying, "They have received my words, they have known who I am, and they have believed on me as their Savior." This is the experience of all God's elect. They may vary in understanding, courage, and many other things, but they have been touched by Jesus. They have his words, and they will inevitably continue to grow in the power of his life and be fruitful for him.[3]

5. Read verses 9–10
    - Emphasize the themes of God's people and God's glory. This is the reason we should pray for other Christians—they are God's and he has set them apart for His glory.
    - Handout question 2: Use this challenging quotation to make application of the principle of pray-

3. Boice, *The Gospel of John, Vol. 4, Peace in Storm,* 1279.

ing for other Christians. Think about Boice's words in the context of personal relationships in a difficult marriage, or with family members and people at church. If we are honest, there are times when we do not look at them as God's children who have the potential to glorify Him. We need to pray for grace to value them because they belong to God, and to want the best for them—that they glorify Him.

6. Read verses 11–16
   Handout question 3.
   - What is the petition in verses 11–16? That God will keep them.
   - You may want to read Psalm 121.
   - What is the significance of Jesus using the term "Holy Father"?
   - What is the resource He gives us? The power of His name.
   - What is the reason Jesus gives for this petition? That we might have His joy in us. Summarize ideas from the following quotations:

John Calvin:

He calls it HIS *joy*, because it was necessary that the disciples should obtain it from him; or, if you choose to express it more briefly, he calls it *his*, because he is the Author, Cause, and Pledge of it; for in us there is nothing but alarm and uneasiness, but in Christ alone there is peace and joy.[4]

4. Calvin, *Calvin's Commentaries, John's Gospel—Vol. II,* 178.

James Boice:

The basis for joy is sound doctrine. When I first began to handle this subject in connection with my exposition of the Book of Philippians, I was surprised to find how many times joy is associated with a mature knowledge of God's Word. . . . What we are talking about in this area is not doctrine in and of itself but rather that experiential knowledge of God's character and commandments that we receive from his Word.[5]

Arthur W. Pink:

This was what the heart of the Saviour craved for His people, and for this He had made full provision. In this Prayer, Christ makes it known that we have been brought into the same position before the Father that He had held, and just in proportion as we consciously enter into it, His joy is fulfilled in us. As the result of His finished work every barrier has been removed.[6]

- Refer to the drawing on the handout and ask the women to share their thoughts about Proverbs 18:10.
- The Scripture Jesus quotes regarding Judas is Psalm 41:9. Ask if anyone has other thoughts about this section.
- The remedy for a lack of joy is a holy life. Sin keeps us from Jesus, and thus from His joy, so next He prays that we will be sanctified by His Word.

5. Boice, *The Gospel of John, Vol. 4, Peace in Storm,* 1295.

6. Arthur W. Pink, *Exposition of the Gospel of John, Vol. 3* (Grand Rapids: Zondervan Publishing House, 1945), 128.

7. Read verse 17
   Handout question 4
   - What is the petition in verse 17? That God will sanctify us in truth.
   - Where do we find truth? His Word.

The Spirit of the Reformation Study Bible on 17:17:

> He wished above all that they should be holy and indicated the only means by which holiness may be attained: "truth." Just as error and deception are the roots of evil, so truth is the root of godliness. Those who wish to advance in holiness must submit not only to Jesus' desire that they be holy, but also to the means he has provided to make them so.[7]

   - Reflect and Pray question 3: Reflect on Psalm 119:36–37. What are some of the worthless, selfish things you need to ask God to turn you from? Compare these with the Worthy One to whom we turn. Discuss this.
   - Emphasize the power of God's Word. Ask volunteers to read the verses on the handout.

8. Handout question 5
   - What are the two threads that run through this passage? The power of God's name and the power of His Word.

9. Handout question 6: How Do We Call on God in Truth?
   - Fill in the blanks for the principles identified in this chapter.

7. *Spirit of the Reformation Study Bible* (Grand Rapids: Zondervan, 2003), 1739.

- Read John 14:13–14. This verse is often misunderstood. It does not teach that we can ask for anything we want. It teaches an important prayer principle: We are to pray in Jesus' name.
- Praying in Jesus' name means asking for what is consistent with His Word and asking on the basis of His merit.
- Read the question from the Westminster Larger Catechism and ask the women to read the answer.

10. Ask for reactions to the Life-giving Prayer story. Ask if anyone has similar memories of someone who prayed for her. Emphasize the value of having specific Scriptures that children and grandchildren hear prayed repeatedly. These are life-giving memories of God's Word that we can give to the next generation. Refer back to the helper verses in chapter one and ask which of the helper characteristics are seen in this story.

3

SANCTIFY: HANDOUT

JOHN 17:6–19

1. Jesus tells us four things about those for whom He prays:
   (1) They are God's: God owns everything by right of ________________. This refers to possession by ________________.
   (2) God gave them to Jesus

John Calvin:

Christ ascribes the cause to the election of God; for he assigns no other difference as the reason why he manifested the name of the Father to some, passing by others, but because they were given to him. . . . Christ declares that the elect always belonged to God. . . . The certainty of that election by free grace lies in this, that he commits to the guardianship of his Son all whom he has elected, that they may not perish.[1]

   (3) Jesus made God's name known to them.
   What is the name of God that Jesus revealed in a unique way? ______________

1. Calvin, *Calvin's Commentaries, John's Gospel—Vol. II*, 170.

All of Jesus' prayers in the Gospels record that He addressed God as Father. There is only one exception. What is it?
In the following prayers, Jesus addressed God as Father.

Matthew 11:25–26
Matthew 26:39, 42
Mark 14:35–36
Luke 23:33–34
John 11:38–44
John 12:12–13, 20–29

(4) They kept God's word

2. James Boice writes about Jesus' words, "I am glorified in them" (v. 10):

> We should pray for others because God is glorified in them. Could it be that you would prefer not to have God glorified in them? I think sometimes, when I hear of frictions that exist between certain Christians and between denominations, that this is precisely what some Christians wish. They do not like the other person or other denomination and hope that these others will do something horrible to show that they themselves are right in having taken the position they have. This is not right. Rather, God has called that one, whoever he is and in whatever circumstances he finds himself, in order that he might do something unique in him that he might bear a valued witness.[2]

3. What is the petition in verses 11–16? ______________

____

2. Boice, *The Gospel of John, Vol. 4, Peace in Storm*, 1286.

"The name of the LORD is a strong tower; the righteous man runs into it and is safe." Proverbs 18:10

4. What is the petition in verse 17? ____________________
   - Where do we find truth?
     Deuteronomy 32:45–47
     Psalm 19:7–11
     Psalm 119:9, 89, 130, 160, 165
     Isaiah 55:11
     Colossians 3:16
     2 Timothy 3:14–17
     Hebrews 4:12
     1 Peter 1:23

5. What are the two threads that run through this passage?
   The power of God's __________________ and the power of His __________________.

6. How do we call on God in truth?
   Approach Him as our ______________.
   Pray in ______________.
   Pray according to His ______________.

Whatever you ask in my name, this I will do, that the Father may be glorified in the Son. If you ask me anything in my name, I will do it. (John 14:13–14)

> Praying in Jesus' name means asking for what is ________________ with his Word and asking on the basis of His ____________________.

Westminster Larger Catechism

Q. 181. Why are we to pray in the name of Christ?
A. The sinfulness of man, and his distance from God by reason thereof, being so great, as that we can have no access into his presence without a mediator; and there being none in heaven or earth appointed to, or fit for, that glorious work but Christ alone, we are to pray in no other name but his only.

The LORD is near to all who call on him,

to all who call on him in truth.

Psalm 145:18

4

UNIFY: LESSON PLAN

John 17:20–26

1. Review: The themes, petitions, and prayer principles in this prayer help us not only to understand this portion of Scripture, they help us to understand all of Scripture. They help us understand prayer. We will continue to see them in other prayers we will study.
   - Handout question 1: You may want to wait until you discuss verses 20–26 to fill in theme 5, petitions 4 and 5, and the last prayer principle.
   - Themes
     (1) God's glory
     (2) God's people
     (3) God's nearness
     (4) God's calling
     (5) God's love
   - Petitions
     (1) Glorify me that I may glorify you.
     (2) Keep them.
     (3) Sanctify them.

(4) Unify them.
(5) I want them to be with me and see my glory.

- How do we call on God in prayer?
  (1) Pray with gratitude for our redemption.
  (2) Pray for His glory.
  (3) Pray according to His eternal plan and purpose.
  (4) Approach Him as our Father.
  (5) Pray in Jesus' name.
  (6) Pray according to His Word.

2. Read verses 20–26

3. v. 20
   - Read the paragraph in the text relating to verse 20. Ask whether there are reactions.
   - Ask: How does it make you feel to know that you stand in a great company of the redeemed that stretches all through history?

4. vv. 21–22
   - Summarize the following quotations to expand on the concept of our union with Christ.

Spirit of the Reformation Study Bible:

There are three great unities proclaimed in Scripture: the unity of the three persons of the Trinity as the one and only God, the unity of the divine and human natures in the one person of Jesus Christ and the unity of Christ and his own people in the fulfillment of redemption.[1]

1. *Spirit of the Reformation Study Bible* (Grand Rapids: Zondervan, 2003), 1732, note on John 14:11.

Spirit of the Reformation Study Bible: "Union with Christ: What Does It Mean to Be 'in Christ'?":

> One of the doctrines most commonly referenced by the New Testament writers was that of believers' union with Christ. This doctrine lies behind the vast majority of their use of phrases such as "in Christ," "in Jesus" and "in him." Reformed theology has tended to recognize two major ideas in this union:
>
> (1) Believers are mystically united to Jesus in a vital way, such that he dwells in them and they in him; and
> (2) Jesus is the representative of believers before the Father, especially in Jesus' death and resurrection.
>
> It has been common to speak of the vital union between Jesus and believers as mystical because the Bible does not define precisely how it takes place or what it entails. . . .
>
> Because believers are joined to Christ in this mystical way, they share not only his experiences but also his very identity, so that the Father looks upon believers as though they were Christ himself, accounting to them Jesus' status and rights.[2]

- This unity that Jesus prays for is foundational to the biblical doctrine of the church.

Unity is the root word of community. The church is a covenant community. This is not a self-determined community. We are not bound together simply by common interests or geography. We are bound together by Christ.

2. Ibid., 1900.

- Handout question 2

Our unity flows out of the union between the Father and Son. We do not create this unity. It is a gift from God. We are adopted into this family.

(1) Read the verses on the handout.

What has He given us so that we can be one? His glory.

(2) Ask: What aspect of His glory has He given us? His character.

NOTE: This idea will be discussed more in the next lesson.

(3) What is the result of our unity? It will be a witness to the world that God sent Jesus and He loves us.
(4) Explain that this prayer will be answered fully when Jesus comes back. The sight of the perfected unity of God's church will be a spectacular sight that even the unbeliever cannot deny. It is our privilege and responsibility to nurture this unity now and to strive to make our marriages and churches a witness of the gospel to the world.
(5) Read the quotation on the handout from the Westminster Confession of Faith.

Often people emphasize only our union with Christ, but Scripture teaches that when we are united to Christ we are also united to one another. This is beautifully expressed in this statement from the Westminster Confession. We actually have communion in each other's gifts and graces. Note the word *obliged*—this is a strong word. Our tendency is to think individualistically, but our union with Christ compels us to think of the mutual good of His family.

- Handout question 1: Petitions—fill in the blank for (4), unity.
- Text, Reflect and Pray question 1: What are some practical ways others have helped you feel united to your church family? How are you challenged to nurture unity in your relationships with others?

In this discussion emphasize that for those who are married, nurturing unity begins in the marriage. We cannot bypass this relationship.

Also refer back to the life-giver/life-taker chart on the handout for lesson one. Emphasize that women's nurturing, relational strengths equip us to bring a wonderful sense of family into the home and church. Discuss the importance of things such as fellowship dinners, baby and bridal showers, meals to the sick, older women helping new mothers, and babysitting for single moms. These seemingly ordinary ministries are extraordinarily profound.

- Read the quotation on the handout from Spurgeon. Ask: What is some of the "dead stuff" that will divide us?
- Text, Reflect and Pray question 2: Discuss these "one anothering" verses. Think about specific applications. Contrast these life-giving actions with the "dead stuff" that Spurgeon mentions.

5. v. 23
   - Summarize this section from the text.
   - What is your reaction to Jesus' statement that God loves us even as He loves Jesus?
   - Handout question 1: Themes—fill in the blank for (5), God's love.
   - You may want to have a time of prayer, thanking God for loving us so. Consider using a hymn of response such as Elizabeth Prentiss' "More Love to Thee, O Christ."
6. v. 24
   - Discuss the amazing fact that Jesus wants to share His home and His glory with us. He wants us there with Him.
   - Handout question 1: Petitions—fill in the blank for (5), with me.
7. vv. 25–26
   - You may want to use this quotation from Arthur Pink to explain Jesus' use of the term "Righteous Father":

> Thus we understand the "O *righteous* Father" here to have a double force. First, God is not only merciful, but just, in glorifying the elect. . . . "He was asking for what *He* was entitled to according to the stipulation of the eternal covenant. *Justice* required that His requests should be granted." (Mr. John Brown). . . . [This is] also to be connected with what follows—"the world hath not known thee." This is very solemn. Christ not only left the world without His intercession, but he turned it over to the justice of the Father. Not

only did Divine *righteousness* bestow heavenly glory on the elect, but Divine *righteousness* refuses to bestow it on the unbelieving world.[3]

- What did you learn from this chapter about love? How are you challenged by the statement: For God so loved that He gave; when we love we take?
- What are your thoughts about biblical love being planted in us and having the capacity to grow? If we are Christians can we ever say, "I can't love that person?" No—we must admit that we refuse to love them, repent, and ask God to fill us with His love. It may be hard, but the power of the gospel can enable us to love even those who have hurt us.

8. How do we call on God in truth?
   - Handout question 1: Fill in the blank.
   - Text, Reflect and Pray question 3: What difference will it make in your life and prayers if you take time to reflect on the eternal perspective of your union with Christ and with other Christians?
   - Refer to the prayer story and ask for reactions.
9. How has John 17 shaped your thoughts about prayer?
   - What are some things you learn in this chapter about yourself? You may want to divide the women into groups and assign each group one section of John 17. Some of the things women may list:

3. Arthur W. Pink, *Exposition of the Gospel of John, Vol. 3* (Grand Rapids: Zondervan Publishing House, 1945), 150.

Jesus prayed for me.
I was chosen by God.
God gave me to Christ.
Jesus has made God's name known to me.
Jesus has given me ability to receive God's Word.
The world hates me.
I am not of the world.
Jesus wants me to have His joy.
Jesus has sent me into the world.
Jesus set Himself apart for my salvation.
Jesus has given me His glory.
Jesus wants me to be united with His other children.
Jesus wants me to be with Him
God loves me as He loves Jesus.

10. Have a time of prayer focused on the love and unity of your church. You may want to have a list of the church leaders and pray for them. Emphasize the importance of unity and our responsibility to diligently guard the unity that Christ has given us.

4

UNIFY: HANDOUT

John 17:20–26

1. Themes, petitions and prayer principles in John 17
   - Themes
     (1) God's ______________________________
     (2) God's ______________________________
     (3) God's ______________________________
     (4) God's ______________________________
     (5) God's ______________________________

   - Petitions
     (1) ____________________ me that I may glorify you.
     (2) __________________________ them.
     (3) __________________________ them.
     (4) __________________________ them.
     (5) I want them to be __________________ and see my glory.

   - How do we call on God in prayer?
     Pray with gratitude for our redemption.
     Pray for His glory.

Pray according to His eternal plan and purpose.
Approach Him as our Father.
Pray in Jesus' name.
Pray according to His Word.
With an eternal perspective, seeing myself _________ in love to Christ and to the great company of the redeemed in all ages.

2. Unity

Our unity flows out of the union between the ________ and _________.
We do not create this unity. It is a gift from God. We are ____________ into this family.

Blessed be the God and Father of our Lord Jesus Christ, who has blessed us in Christ with every spiritual blessing in the heavenly places, even as he chose us in him before the foundation of the world, that we should be holy and blameless before him. In love he predestined us for adoption as sons through Jesus Christ. (Eph. 1:3–5)

God arranged the members in the body, each one of them, as he chose. (1 Cor. 12:18).

What has He given us so that we can be one?
What is the result of our unity? It will be a witness to the world that God sent ________ and He _____________ us.

Westminster Confession of Faith, Chapter XXVI: Of the Communion of Saints

All saints, that are united to Jesus Christ their head, by His Spirit, and by faith, have fellowship with Him in His grace, sufferings, death, resurrection, and glory: and, being united to one another in love, they have communion in each other's gifts and graces, and are obliged to the performance of such duties, public and private, as do conduce to their mutual good, both in the inward and outward man.

Charles Spurgeon:

May the Lord bless us, dear friends, as a Church, make us one, and keep us so; for it will be the dead stuff among us that will make the divisions. It is the living children of God that make the unity, it is the living ones that are bound together. . . . As for those of you who are joined with us in visible fellowship, and are not one with Christ, may the Lord save you with His great salvation, and His shall be the praise.[1]

1. Charles Haddon Spurgeon, *The Treasury of the Bible, New Testament, Vol. 2* (Grand Rapids: Zondervan Publishing House, 1962), 615.

The Lord is near to all who call on him,
to all who call on him in truth.
Psalm 145:18

5

NEARNESS: LESSON PLAN

Exodus 32–34

NOTE: There is a lot of information in this lesson. If your schedule allows, you may want to divide it into two lessons. Read the chapter several times and determine what you want to emphasize. The handout has wonderful quotations from sermons by two nineteenth-century Scottish pastors, John M'Laurin and Alexander Maclaren. Having these on the handout will allow women to continue to read and reflect on them.

1. Review
   - Refer to the handout for lesson one, question 1, and read the quotation from Edmund Clowney. The more we understand the "one great story" of the Bible, the more we know how to pray according to God's plan and purpose. As we look at Moses' prayer, it is thrilling to see the connections with the foundational realities we saw in chapter one and the themes and petitions we saw in John 17.

- Ask: What are the first two foundational realities we saw in Genesis 1? God's Word is our authority. God's glory is our purpose.
- Emphasize that our authority and purpose are the fundamental struggles we see in Exodus 32–34.
- What are the themes we identified in John 17? God's glory, people, nearness, calling, and love.

2. Text, Reflect and Pray question 1: Think about the themes and petitions in John 17. Read Exodus 32–34 and reflect on the similarities. Ask: What are some of the similarities you saw? A brief discussion of this question can help focus on the material to be covered.

3. What are the two struggles involved in our nearness to God?
   - Handout question 1

The first struggle with the world is the struggle for our justification. Jesus won this battle on the cross.

The second battle is for our sanctification. This is an ongoing battle. The issues in this battle are our authority and our purpose.

- Read the questions from the Westminster Shorter Catechism and ask the women to read the answers. Note that justification is the work of God. He declares us to be justified on the basis of the merit of Christ. We are passive. Sanctification is a process in which we are enabled to increasingly turn from sin and turn to Christ. In John 17 Jesus prayed for our sanctification, and He continues to do so.

- Moses' petitions in Exodus 32–34 have to do with our sanctification. As we examine these petitions, we need to think on two levels: our own sanctification and our intercession for the sanctification of others.

4. The Israelites' declaration, "All the words that the Lord has spoken *we will do*" stands in contrast with the "*I wills*" of God. Refer to Genesis 3:15 and the covenant promise verses listed on the handout for lesson one. God's sovereign "I will" shows us that He does for us what we cannot do for ourselves. Whereas we do have a responsibility for obedience in our sanctification, we are dependent on the power of the gospel (Phil. 2:13). There is one way of justification and sanctification—Jesus. The Israelites were vulnerable because they were depending on self-effort.

5. Refer to the text and read Acts 7:38–40 and 1 Corinthians 10:5–7, 14.
   - "Man must have an object, and when he turns from the true God, he at once craves a false one. . . . It is only as our affections are set upon Him, as we are in daily communion with Him, that our hearts are kept from idols."[1]
   - "Man is the only creature who lives on the earth that was originally created with faculties capable of apprehending God, and with a sentiment of veneration for Him. . . . The loss of the knowledge of the true God, to a creature endowed with religious faculties, must

1. Arthur W. Pink, *Gleanings in Exodus* (Chicago: Moody Press, 1971), 316.

result in subjective idolizing. . . . [This explains] the universality of idolatry."[2]

- Ask someone to read Jeremiah 17:23: "Yet they did not listen or incline their ear, but stiffened their neck, that they might not hear and receive instruction."

Note the connection between being stubborn and rebellious and hearing and receiving the instruction of God's Word. Also note that in Acts 7:38–40 the Word is referred to as "living oracles."

- Reflect and Pray question 2: What are some idols Christian women struggle with? Emphasize the importance of hearing and receiving the instruction of God's Word as we identify and battle our idols.

6. Near or far
   - Read Exodus 25:8–9. Why were they to build a tabernacle? So God would dwell among them.

The tabernacle represented God's presence among them, the promise of the covenant. God gave specific instructions about the construction of the tabernacle. We can only approach God according to His Word. Everything in the tabernacle pointed to Jesus.

When the Israelites turned to another god, they forfeited the blessing of nearness. God threatened to withdraw His presence. At issue is the placement of the tabernacle. All of Moses' petitions are focused on pleading for God's presence among them.

2. Ibid., 320.

7. The First Petition: Remember your promise (32:13).
   - Read 32:1. The people refer to Moses as the one who brought them out of Egypt. How quickly they forgot the gracious words of 19:3–6. Read this passage.
   - Read 32:4. They attribute their deliverance to the golden calf.
   - Read 32:7–10. The people rejected Jehovah. He now refers to them not as "my people," but as "your people." This terrible separation is at the heart of Moses' petitions. He is pleading for God to tabernacle among them.
   - His first petition is the ground of his plea: your promise. It is a promise of grace, which shows us God's character.
   - Handout question 2: Read the quotation.

They were *God's* people—His by redemption. They were His purchased property. Unworthy, unthankful, unholy; but yet, the Lord's redeemed. Blessed, glorious, heart-melting fact: O may the realization of it create within us a greater hatred of sin and a deeper appreciation of the precious blood of the Lamb.[3]

8. The Second Petition: Forgive their sins (32:32).
   - Summarize 32:15–29.
   - The broken tablets pictured the broken covenant.
   - *ESV Study Bible*: "Moses' intercession on behalf of the people results in the Lord's relenting from consuming them entirely. . . . However, Moses himself

3. Ibid., 322.

will be a means of judgment on some of the people (Ex. 32:26–29), and the Lord will judge them further through a plague (v. 35)."[4]

- It is difficult for us to understand this passage, but we must remember that the justice of God must be satisfied. Sin must be punished. Our hearts should overflow with gratitude that Jesus satisfied God's justice for us.
- It is significant to note that the one who used the sword then prayed for them.
- Read 32:30–32.
- Handout question 3: Read the quotation. If you want to explain the reference to the Book of Life, use the following:

> The "book of life" is often spoken of in Scripture . . . (Ps. 69:28; Dan. 12:1; Phil. 4:3; Rev. 3:5). The allusion is to the citizens' roll (Ps. 87:6). Those whose names are written there have the privileges of citizenship, and as it is the "book of life" (or "of the living"), life in the widest sense is secured to them. To blot someone out of it, therefore, is to cut a man off from fellowship in the city of God, and from participation in life.[5]

9. The Third Petition: Show me your ways that I may know you (33:13–14).
   - Read Exodus 33:1–6. The crisis continues. It is not entrance to the Promised Land that is in question. It is the nearness of God.

4. *English Standard Version Study Bible* (Wheaton, IL: Crossway Bibles, 2008), 197.
5. Alexander Maclaren, *Expositions of Holy Scripture* (Charleston, SC: BiblioBazaar, 2006), 459. Note: No date is given for the original publication.

- Read Exodus 33:7–11. This section seems to be off topic, but it is a reinforcement of the primary point of the passage: Will the tabernacle be "outside the camp" or will it be central. Some prefer God at a distance, but Moses was pleading for God's nearness.
- Read 33:12–14.
- This was a time of uncertainty. "In the strong metaphor of the context, God was making up His mind on His course, and Israel was waiting with hushed breath. . . . It was not the entrance of the nation into the promised land which was in doubt, but the manner of their guidance, and the penalties of their idolatry."[6]
- Handout question 4: Read the explanation.

Remembering that our relationship with God begins with Him fosters a spirit of humility and gratitude.

God's response is gracious, but Moses pleads for more. He keeps pushing heavenward to claim the covenant blessings for the people, foreshadowing Jesus' prayer for us in John 17.

10. The Fourth Petition: Your presence with *us* (33:15–17)
    - Read 33:15–17.
    - Handout question 5: Read the quotation.
11. The Fifth Petition: Show me your glory (33:18)

> This great event derives additional significance and grandeur from the place in which it stands. It follows the hideous act

6. Ibid., 470.

> of idolatry in which the levity and sinfulness of Israel reached their climax. . . . Then comes this wonderful advance in the progress of divine revelation.[7]

- Ask: What does God say that He will show Moses? The goodness of His character.
- Use the text to summarize the significance of God putting Moses in the cleft of the rock.
- Read Exodus 34:6–7.

Spirit of the Reformation Study Bible:

> God's mercy was still proclaimed for Israel despite her dismal failure. . . . Because of God's love and faithfulness, he would not abandon his people, but would dwell among them in his tabernacle.[8]

Exodus 34:6–7 is an amazing explanation of the glory of God's character. Refer to the text, chapter two, and remind the women of the external and internal aspects of God's glory. There have been spectacular visible manifestations of God's glory in Exodus, but here we see a revelation of the glory of His character.

He first proclaims His name. See John 17:6, 11, 12. He reveals His name Jehovah, translated Lord, showing that He is a covenant God who lives in personal relationship with His people. This name points to Jesus, for it is only through Jesus that we can have a relationship with the Father. Every attribute He reveals is a description of Jesus.

7. Ibid., 477.
8. *Spirit of the Reformation Study Bible* (Grand Rapids: Zondervan, 2003), 151.

- Handout question 6: Read the quotation.
- As stated in the text, this passage formed the foundation for Hebrew piety. The passage is repeated frequently in the Old Testament to shape appeals to God in prayer.

Ask volunteers to read the passages on the handout.

- This passage is central to our sanctification. It gives definition to reflecting God's glory. Becoming merciful, gracious, loving, and forgiving is the result of living in intimate relationship with Him.

12. The Sixth Petition: Take us for your inheritance (34:9)
    - Use the quotation in the text from Pink and the final section, "Covenant Renewal."
    - Read the "true woman" statement in the text.
    - Handout question 7: Read 2 Corinthians 3:18; 4:6.
    - We see the glory of God in the face of Jesus Christ through His revelation of Himself in His Word. We are sanctified by the Word (John 17:17) because as we gaze at the glory of His character we are transformed into His image.
    - Read the quotation on the handout. Emphasize that we do not just act more merciful, gracious, loving, and forgiving. The gospel is transformational. We are changed from life-takers to life-givers.
13. In the remainder of Exodus, the Israelites build the tabernacle according to God's instructions.
    - Read 40:34–38.

- But what about the placement of the tabernacle? Was it near or far?
- In Numbers 2, God instructs the people to camp around the tabernacle by families. The tabernacle is the central, defining, unifying characteristic of the community. God's presence among them is a constant reminder of His mercy and pardoning love to them. His glory is what will distinguish and unite them (John 17:22–23).
- In John 1:14 we read that the Word (Jesus) came and tabernacled among us. Later, in 1 Corinthians 3:16, God's people (His church) are said to be His temple. In 1 Corinthians 6:19, individual believers are referred to as His temple. Christ dwells in us—this is extraordinary, transforming grace.

14. Handout question 8: Fill in the blank.

15. There are many ways to make application of this lesson. Three suggestions:

    (1) At times we live with, and sometimes lead, stiff-necked people. What difference will it make if we pray "Show me your glory" rather than giving God a list of ways to change them?

    Suggestions: Often our focus is on how others need to change. But if we ask God to cause the beauty of His mercy, grace, love, and forgiveness to flow to others through us, we will change. This is sanctification.

    (2) Reflect and Pray question 4: What do you learn from Moses about being an intercessor? Some suggestions:

Exodus 32:7–9: Desire the good of others above self-advancement.
Exodus 32:13: Pray on the basis of God's Word and His character.
Exodus 32:32: An intercessor's love is so deep that she would take the place of the other if she could, but she knows the one for whom she prays needs Jesus.
Exodus 33:13–17: The intercessor understands that the real need is not a change of circumstances; the person needs to know God's nearness in her circumstances.
Exodus 33:18: The intercessor knows her own need to continually look at the glory of God in Christ in order to persevere in loving and praying for others.

In a parallel account in Deuteronomy 9:13–21, we see the intensity of Moses' emotion as he prayed for the people. Read this account.

(3) Review the answers to "How do we call on God in truth?" and ask what difference this makes in the women's prayer lives. This is not a formula to follow. These are principles that should inform our thinking about prayer.

5

NEARNESS: HANDOUT

Exodus 32–34

1. What are the two struggles involved in our nearness to God?
   The first struggle is for our ____________________.
   The second struggle is for our ____________________.

Westminster Shorter Catechism

Q. 33. What is justification?
A. Justification is an act of God's free grace, wherein he pardoneth all our sins, and accepteth us as righteous in his sight only for the righteousness of Christ imputed to us, and received by faith alone.

Q. 35. What is sanctification?
A. Sanctification is the work of God's free grace, whereby we are renewed in the whole man after the image of God, and are enabled more and more to die unto sin, and live unto righteousness.

2. The First Petition: Remember your promise (32:13)

The appeal is not based on anything in the people. God is not asked to forgive because of the people's repentance or faith.

> True, these are the conditions under which we receive his pardon, but they are not the reasons that he gives it. Nor does Moses appeal to any sacrifices that had been conceived and offered to placate God. But he goes deeper than all such pleas and lays hold, with sublime confidence, on God's own nature as his all-powerful plea.[1]

3. The Second Petition: Forgive their sins (32:32)

> We must keep [Moses'] severity in mind if we would rightly judge his self-sacrificing devotion, and his self-sacrificing devotion if we would rightly judge his severity. No words of ours can make more sublime his utter self-abandonment for the sake of the people among whom he had just been flaming in wrath, and smiting like a destroying angel. That was a great soul which had for its poles such justice and such love . . . [that was] ready to give up everything for the sake of its objects. . . . Moses was a true type of Christ in that act of supreme self-sacrifice; and all the heroism, the identification of himself with his people, the love which willingly accepts death, that makes his prayer one of the greatest deeds on the page of history, are repeated in infinitely sweeter, more heart-subduing fashion in the story of the Cross.[2]

4. The Third Petition: Show me your ways that I may know you (33:13–14)

Moses bases this petition on God's knowledge of him, not his knowledge of God: "You have said, 'I know you by name.' " Moses was aware that the only reason he knew God was that God first

1. Alexander Maclaren, *Expositions of Holy Scripture* (Charleston, SC: BiblioBazaar, 2006), 613.

2. Ibid., 459–60.

knew him. On the basis of this sovereignly initiated relationship—a relationship of grace—he asks God for guidance and intimacy. And then he reminds God of the people's grace relationship with Him.

5. The Fourth Petition: Your presence with *us* (33:15–17)

> Moses has learned that God's heart must long to reveal its depth of mercy, and therefore he pleads that even sinful Israel should not be left by God, in order that some light from His face may strike into a dark world. . . . The divine answer yields unconditionally to the request, and rests the reason for so doing wholly on the relation between God and Moses. . . . We see in [this] a foreshadowing of our great High-priest. He, too, knits Himself so closely with us, both by the assumption of our manhood and by the identity of loving sympathy, that He accepts nothing from the Father's hand for Himself alone. He, too, presents Himself before God, and says "I and Thy people" . . . His prayer for them prevails, and the reason for its prevalence is God's delight in Him.[3]

6. The Fifth Petition: Show me your glory (33:18)

In this description of God's character we see

> The two qualities of merciful forgiveness and retributive justice. . . . In Jesus these two elements, pardoning love and retributive justice, wondrously meet. . . . Jesus has manifested the divine mercifulness; Jesus has borne the burden of sin and the weight of the divine Justice. . . . The most awe-kindling manifestation of the God "that will by no means clear the guilty," are fused into one, when we "behold the Lamb of

3. Ibid., 473.

> God that taketh away the sin of the world" . . . the answer to a great sin. . . . So for us all Christ is the full and final revelation of God's grace.[4]

Exodus 34:6–7 was used throughout the Old Testament to shape the appeal of God's people in their prayers:

Numbers 14:18
Nehemiah 9:17
Psalm 86:15
Psalm 103:8
Psalm 145:8
Joel 2:13
Jonah 4:2
Nahum 1:3

7. The Sixth Petition: Take us for your inheritance (34:9)

> For God, who said, "Let light shine out of darkness," has shone in our hearts to give the light of the knowledge of the glory of God in the face of Jesus Christ. (2 Cor. 4:6)

> And we all, with unveiled face, beholding the glory of the Lord, are being transformed into the same image from one degree of glory to another. (2 Cor. 3:18)

> The chief effects of the cross of Christ, and which shew most of its glory, are its inward effects on the souls of men. . . . [This] glory produces powerful effects wherever it shines. They who behold this glory are transformed into the same image. . . . It melts cold and frozen hearts. . . . It gives

4. Ibid., 479–80.

eyes to the blind. . . . It is the light of life. . . . Its energy is beyond the force of thunder, and it is more mild than the dew on the tender grass. . . . It communicates glory to all that behold it aright. It gives them a glorious robe of righteousness; their God is their glory; it calls them to glory and virtue; it gives them the spirit of God and of glory; it gives them joy unspeakable and full of glory here, and an exceeding great and eternal weight of glory hereafter.[5]

8. How do we call on God in truth? Appeal on the basis of His ______________.

5. *Precious Seed, Discourses by Scottish Worthies* (Birmingham, AL: Solid Ground Christian Books, 2007, taken from 1877 edition by John Grieg & Son, Edinburgh), 34–36.

The LORD is near to all who call on him,

to all who call on him in truth.

Psalm 145:18

6

FORGIVEN: LESSON PLAN

Psalm 51

1. Review
   - What are the first two foundational realities we see in Genesis 1? God's Word is our authority and God's glory is our purpose.
   - These are the realities David struggled with in the events that led to his prayer in Psalm 51. They are the realities we face every day. In every situation we must ask: What is my authority in determining how to react? What is my purpose?
   - In the last lesson, when Moses prayed "Show me Your glory," what did God show him? The glory of His character. Read Exodus 34:6–7. It is thrilling to see the connection between this passage and Psalm 51.
2. Read or summarize the first two paragraphs of the text.
   - Emphasize that the context of this prayer shows us that a mature Christian can fall into grievous sin. Also, the secret sins of the heart are just as grievous as our outward behavior.

3. The Context
   - Read or summarize 2 Samuel 11–12:15.
   - Many commentators believe that Psalm 32 may be the fulfillment of the promise in Psalm 51:13.

James Boice writes:

> The relationship of the psalms is close. Both seem to have grown out of the same moral failure on David's part, though Psalm 51 is more intense and personal and seems to have been written close to the event, while Psalm 32 is more reflective and was probably written later. It may be that Psalm 32, which is identified as a *maskil* (possibly meaning "instruction"), is a fulfillment of the promise David makes to "teach transgressors your ways" in Psalm 51:13.[1]

You may want to read Psalm 32. Especially note verses 3 and 4. God's hand was heavy on David, preparing him for Nathan's visit. Confrontation will not help one trapped in sin until God breaks him.

David was so blind to his sin that he did not even get the point of Nathan's story until Nathan said, "You are the man!" Emphasize the great danger of the deceptiveness of sin. Often we deflect our own guilt just as David did—he was outraged at the actions of the rich man rather than seeing his own sin.

- What did Nathan point to as the root cause of David's actions? Second Samuel 12:9. When God's Word is not our authority, our purpose becomes

1. James Montgomery Boice, *An Expositional Commentary, Psalms, Vol. 2, Psalms 42–106* (Grand Rapids: Baker Books, 1996), 426.

our pleasure. This is not just a behavior problem; it is a heart problem.

- Handout question 1: Read and discuss the quotation.

4. Repentance and Faith
   - Refer to the text. Read the questions from the Westminster Shorter Catechism and ask the women to read the answers.
   - Emphasize that repentance and faith are saving and sanctifying graces. As we grow in Christ, repentance goes deeper and faith goes higher.
   - Read the *Spirit of the Reformation Study Bible* article, "Repentance: How Sorry Do I Have to Be?"

Faith and repentance are mutual conditions for salvation. . . . Both are gifts of God that result from regeneration—the heart set free from sin gratefully conforms to the command to repent and believe the gospel. Repentance, whether a firstfruit of God's work of regeneration . . . or a mature response to sin . . . is a gift of God accompanying both saving faith . . . and the ongoing faith flowing from the Holy Spirit. . . . One cannot turn to God in faith without first turning from sin in repentance.[2]

- Read Handout question 2.

The ESV Study Bible note on Revelation 3:20:

I stand at the door and knock, not as a homeless transient seeking shelter but as the master of the house, expecting alert servants to respond immediately to his signal and welcome his

2. *Spirit of the Reformation Study Bible* (Grand Rapids: Zondervan, 2003), 857.

entrance. . . . To the one who opens the door, Christ will come in and will eat with him, a picture of close personal fellowship.[3]

5. Read Psalm 51

    - Paul David Tripp:

You haven't really understood Psalm 51 until you have realized that every word of this penitential psalm cries for Jesus. Every promise embedded in this psalm looks for fulfillment in Jesus. Every need of Psalm 51 reaches out for help in Jesus. Every commitment of Psalm 51 honors Jesus. The sin that's at the heart of this psalm will only ever find its cure in the grace of Jesus. . . . Psalm 51 is Immanuel's hymn. The forgiveness of Psalm 51 rests on the shoulders of the One whose name would be Immanuel.[4]

6. The Basis of the Appeal: verses 1–2
    - Summarize this section.
    - Handout question 3: The basis of David's appeal was God's Word.

Fill in the blanks: Pray according to His Word (chapter three), make our appeal on the basis of His character (chapter 5).

- David owned his sin and called it what it was: *my* transgressions, *my* iniquity, *my* sin. Often we hear public figures who have been caught in sin call it a profound mistake, or a serious indiscretion. Violation of God's law is sin.
- Recognizing our sin and our sinfulness is essential to growth in grace. You may want to read Romans 3:23.

3. *English Standard Version Study Bible* (Wheaton, IL: Crossway Bibles, 2008), 2469.
4. Paul David Tripp, *Whiter Than Snow* (Wheaton, IL: Crossway Books, 2008), 102.

Spirit of the Reformation Study Bible note on Romans 3:23:

A poignant description of the consequence of sin. Created in the image of the glorious God (Ge 1:26–27), human beings have exchanged God's glory for idolatry (Ro 1:23) and distorted their divine image. Only grace through faith renews and restores that lost glory.[5]

7. The Heart of the Broken: verses 3–5
   - It is frightening to realize how we can deceive ourselves. Sin slowly blinds us to the truth about ourselves. What are some ways we deceive ourselves? Suggestions: Blaming others for our situation (My husband is so indifferent and this coworker is so understanding and kind. He's just a friend). Rationalizing (I know God doesn't want me to be so unhappy, so it must be all right for me to . . .).
   - Handout question 4: Ask volunteers to read the verses.

You may want to discuss preventive measures we can take to keep ourselves from being deceived. Suggestions: The means of grace—Bible study, prayer, worship, the sacraments, and fellowship are the means God has provided to keep us near Him. Emphasize the need for Christian friends who watch, pray for, and confront each other.

Read the quotations by Paul David Tripp.

- Read and discuss the "true woman" statement on the handout.
- The next section is a wonderful testimony of faith. David believes that the blessings of grace flow beyond the curse of sin.

5. *Spirit of the Reformation Study Bible*, 1815.

Before thinking about the future of the forgiven, you may want to spend a few minutes in silent confession. Read 1 John 1:9. After a time of silence, sing verses 1 and 3 of *Joy to the World.*

8. The Future of the Forgiven, verses 6–12
    - Consider David's requests in these verses. How would you summarize these requests?

Do you see any correlation between the blessings David requests and Jesus' prayer in John 17? Jesus' petitions—keep them, sanctify them, unify them, I want them with me—are the things for which David longed.

- Handout question 5: Read the quotations.
- Discuss verse 8. It is important for women to understand the sovereign love of God in our times of crushing. He crushes in order to draw us near. Use Romans 8:28 and emphasize that He works *all* things—not some things—together to conform us to His image.
- Read the "true woman" statement in the text and ask for reactions.

9. The Ministry of the Forgiven, verses 13–17
    - Ask for reactions to this section in the text. Ask: How have you seen women being good stewards of their stories of grace? Suggestion: Many women who have had abortions turn that experience into a ministry by working in crisis pregnancy centers. Being a good steward of our stories of grace does not necessarily mean that we tell the details of the experience, especially if it would expose the sin of someone else. But it

does mean that if we have experienced God's forgiveness we will be willing to lovingly help other sinners find the way back.

10. The Heart of the Forgiven, verses 18–19

    - Charles Spurgeon:

Zion was David's favourite spot, whereon he had hoped to erect a temple. . . . He felt he had hindered the project of honouring the Lord there as he desired, but he prayed God still to let the place of his ark be glorious, and to establish his worship and his worshipping people . . . but we believe he had a more spiritual meaning, and prayed for the prosperity of the Lord's cause and people. He had done mischief by his sin, and had, as it were pulled down her walls; he, therefore, implores the Lord to undo the evil, and establish his church. . . . There is surely no grace in us if we do not feel for the church of God, and take a lasting interest in its welfare.[6]

    - Spurgeon (v. 16):

The Psalmist was so illuminated as to see far beyond the symbolic ritual; his eye of faith gazed with delight upon the actual atonement. . . . He knew that no form of burnt sacrifice was a satisfactory propitiation. His deep soul-need made him look from the type to the antitype, from the external rite to the inward grace.[7]

11. Read 2 Samuel 12:15–25
    - There are often consequences to our sin even though we are forgiven, but being forsaken by God is not a

6. C. H. Spurgeon, *The Treasury of David, Vol. 1, Psalms 1–57* (Grand Rapids: Zondervan Publishing House, 1974), 407.

7. Ibid.

consequence for those He gave to Jesus. "The LORD loved him" (v. 24) is a sweet statement of assurance. Jedidiah means *loved by the LORD*. Note that the name God uses here is Jehovah (translated LORD), which is His personal name of covenant faithfulness to His own.

- What evidences of repentance, faith, and forgiveness do you see in David?

  v. 20: He went to church and worshiped.

  v. 23: He had assurance that the child was in heaven and that he would go there too.

  v. 24: David is no longer self-absorbed. He comforts his wife.

12. Handout question 6: How do we call on God in truth? With a repentant and believing heart.

13. Discuss the Life-giving Prayer story.

14. The Read and Reflect section is very personal, but you may want to refer to it and ask whether anyone has something to share.

6

FORGIVEN: HANDOUT

Psalm 51

1. What did Nathan identify as the root cause of David's sin in 2 Samuel 12:9?

Paul David Tripp:

You and I will only ever be holy by God's definition if we put the moral fences where God puts them. We tend to put the fences at the boundary of behavior. . . . Christ draws the fences in much closer. He calls for us to fence our hearts because he knows that it's only when we fence the heart that we'll willingly and successfully stay inside God-appointed behavioral fences. . . . By God's grace, determine to fight the battle of thought and desire, knowing full well that it's only when you win this battle that you can be successful in the battle of behavior. And rest assured that when you fight this battle you aren't fighting alone, but your Lord wages war on your behalf.[1]

1. Tripp, *Whiter Than Snow*, 123–25.

2. Repentance

> Those whom I love, I reprove and discipline, so be zealous and repent. Behold, I stand at the door and knock. If anyone hears my voice and opens the door, I will come in to him and eat with him, and he with me. (Rev. 3:19–20)

The Westminster Confession of Faith:

> Men ought not to content themselves with a general repentance, but it is every man's duty to endeavor to repent of his particular sins, particularly. (WCF 15.5)

3. The basis of David's appeal was God's _____________.

This prayer illustrates two of the principles we have identified as ways we call on God in truth:

(1) Pray according to God's _________________.
(2) Make our appeal on the basis of His __________.

4. Scripture warns us to be careful of the deception of sin.
   Deuteronomy 11:16
   Isaiah 44:20
   Jeremiah 49:16
   Obadiah 1:3
   Hebrews 3:13

Tripp:

> Sin is deceitful. . . . Sin always first deceives the person who is sinning the sin. . . . We need help in order to see ourselves with accuracy. . . . We need a ministry of two communities in order

to see ourselves with the kind of surgical clarity with which David speaks in this psalm. First, we need community with God. . . . Through the convicting ministry of the Holy Spirit we begin to see ourselves with accuracy and become willing to own up to what we see. But the Spirit uses instruments, and this is where the second community comes in. God employs people in the task of giving sight to other people.[2]

Tripp:

The desire to be God rather than to serve God lies at the bottom of every sin that anyone has ever committed. . . . Sin is rooted in my unwillingness to find joy in living my life under the authority of, and for the glory of, Another. Sin is rooted in my desire to live for me. It's driven by my propensity to indulge my every feeling, satisfy my every desire, and meet my every need.[3]

The true woman continually searches her heart by asking:

- Is God's Word my authority?
- Is God's glory my purpose?

5. The Future of the Forgiven

Charles Spurgeon comments on verse 7:

Scarcely does Holy Scripture contain a verse more full of faith than this. Considering the nature of the sin, and the deep sense

2. Ibid., 133.
3. Ibid., 81.

the Psalmist had of it, it is a glorious faith to be able to see in the blood sufficient, nay, all-sufficient merit entirely to purge it away. Considering also the deep, natural inbred corruption which David saw and experienced within, it is a miracle of faith that he could rejoice in the hope of perfect purity in his inward parts. Yet, be it added, the faith is no more than the word warrants, than the blood of atonement encourages, than the promise of God deserves. O that some reader may take heart, even now while smarting under sin, to do the Lord the honour to rely thus confidently on the finished sacrifice of Calvary and the infinite mercy there revealed.[4]

Spurgeon on verse 8:

He is requesting a great thing; he seeks joy for a sinful heart, music for crushed bones. Preposterous prayer anywhere but at the throne of God! Preposterous there most of all but for the cross where Jehovah Jesus bore our sins in his own body on the tree.[5]

6. How do we call on God in truth? With a ____________ and ____________ heart.

4. Spurgeon, *Treasury of David*, 404.
5. Ibid. 404.

The LORD is near to all who call on him,

to all who call on him in truth.

Psalm 145:18

7

FORGIVING: LESSON PLAN

ACTS 7:54–60

1. Review
   - What were Jesus' requests for us in John 17? That God will keep us, sanctify us, unify us, and take us to be with Him.
   - What does unforgiveness do to our relationships? It divides us. Forgiveness is essential to unity.
   - What does Jesus give us so that we can have unity in our relationships? His glory—the glory of His character. Forgiveness is one aspect of His goodness (Ex. 34:6–7).
   - It is exciting to see the connections among all the prayers we are studying. They are tied together by themes and concepts that tell the redemption story. They all ultimately tell us about Jesus. Jesus is our pattern and our power to become forgivers.

2. Use the text and the information below to work through each passage. This lesson may be difficult for some women, especially if they are struggling to forgive someone who has hurt them severely. Emphasize that it may take hard work over a period of time, but the power of the gospel makes it possible to forgive. Pray for wisdom and sensitivity so that this will be an encouragement for women struggling with forgiveness. Hold out the hope of the gospel to empower us.

3. Matthew 18:21–35
   - Ask someone to read this passage. You may want to ask some women ahead of time to prepare to act out the parable.
   - Refer to the text, and ask someone to read the quotation from Joe Novenson.
   - Reflect and Pray question 2: What are some losses people may incur when they forgive? Ideas: We give up inflicting humiliation and pain on our offender. We lose the opportunity to receive sympathy from others or to vindicate ourselves. It may mean admitting that we are not completely innocent in the situation. Ultimately, it means losing self.

Handout question 1: Fill in the blanks—deny, save, loses. *ESV Study Bible*:

Crucifixion is a shocking metaphor for discipleship. A disciple must deny himself (die to self-will), take up his cross (embrace God's will, no matter the cost), and follow Christ."[1]

1. *English Standard Version Study Bible* (Wheaton, IL: Crossway Bibles, 2008), 1841.

Emphasize that dying to self is a process, and so is forgiveness. The losses we incur do not compare with what we gain. We gain Christ; we gain life.

- Handout question 2: Read Psalm 51:10 together. This is part of David's prayer of repentance. How would this prayer also apply to one who needs to forgive someone? God is the one who gives us a clean, forgiving heart.
- Refer to Matthew 18:35. Forgiveness must be from the heart. We saw in the last chapter that repentance is also a heart issue. Repentance *and* forgiveness are graces given to us by the Holy Spirit. They both are fruit of the gospel. We should pray for these graces.

4. Prayers from the cross
    - These are poignant passages. Ask volunteers to read each one: Matthew 26:36–42; Matthew 27:46; Luke 23:34.
    - *ESV Study Bible* note on Matthew 27:46:

> Jesus quotes Ps. 22:1. . . . Jesus probably has in mind the remainder of the psalm as well, which moves on to a cry of victory (Ps. 22:21–31); and he expresses faith, calling God "my God." Surely he knows why he is dying, for this was the purpose of his coming to earth. . . . And surely his cry, uttered with a loud voice, is expressing, not bewilderment at his plight, but witness to the bystanders, and through them to the world, that he was experiencing God-forsakenness not for anything in himself but for the salvation of others.[2]

2. Ibid., 1886.

- Ask: What is your reaction to these prayers of our Savior? What do you learn from them?
- Spend time in prayer—give women time to write their prayers, have a time of silent prayer, or pray together.

5. Acts 6
    - What do we learn about Stephen in Acts 6:1–8? He was full of faith, full of the Holy Spirit, full of grace and power.

What does that tell you about him? He was a recipient of God's grace. He was empty of self. This kind of maturity indicates that he lived a life of repentance and forgiveness. His purpose was God's glory, and his authority was God's Word.

- Summarize verses 9–14. Read verse 15.

Handout question 3: Read the responsive reading and ask: What does it mean for our faces to be radiant? Do our countenances reflect our heart? In Genesis 4:5 we read that Cain was angry and his face fell (some translations say his countenance fell). Psalm 10:4 speaks of a haughty countenance and Proverbs 25:23 speaks of an angry countenance (NASB). When people are full of the peace and joy of the Holy Spirit, there is radiance to their countenance. This is a reflected radiance, one that is ours only as we live in the light of God's glory.

Read the "true woman" statement on the handout. Emphasize that sometimes forgiveness takes a long time.

6. Acts 7:1–53
    - Stephen's defense is a magnificent history lesson. Here is another reason his face was like that of an

angel: He knew God's Word and he knew that it is about Jesus.

You may want to refer to Luke 24:13–48. As two of the disciples walked to Emmaus after the crucifixion, they looked sad (v. 17). In v. 31 they recognized the "stranger" as Jesus. Note verse 32: Their sad hearts became burning hearts when Jesus taught them the Scriptures. In verses 44–49, He showed them that all of the Scriptures are about Him.

- Ask: How does Stephen begin his sermon in chapter 7? He begins with God's glory. He respectfully refers to his questioners as "brothers and fathers."

Stephen's sermon is an amazing review of the redemption story. In this sermon we see the five themes from John 17.

Handout question 4: Fill in the blanks—glory, people, nearness, calling, love.

Divide the passage into sections and ask volunteers to read it. Encourage the women to imagine themselves being in the crowd and hearing Stephen. As you read, identify the themes from John 17. Examples:

vv. 2–8: God's glory
vv. 2–3: God's people
vv. 9, 30–34, 40–47: nearness
vv. 3, 34–36: calling

God's love is woven all through the sermon. The astounding fact that the God of glory *appeared*—that He made Himself known—is an act of love.

- Verse 51: Here we see the contrast between the heart of Stephen and the hearts of the Jews who opposed him. Stephen was full of the Holy Spirit; they resisted the Spirit.

7. Acts 7:54–60
   - Verse 54: We see the contrast between the behavior of Stephen and that of the people. Whatever is in the heart shows up on our faces and in our behavior.
   - Verse 55: Stephen looked into heaven. In Matthew 14:28–33 Peter walked on top of water as long as he kept his eyes on Jesus. When he looked at the situation he began to sink. Forgiveness is as unnatural to our fallen nature as walking on water, but it is possible because of Jesus.

We keep our eyes on Jesus by reading the Word, prayer, worship, and fellowship. We cannot overstate the need to tenaciously stay in the Word when the stones are whizzing toward us.

- Verse 56: You may want to read Daniel 7:13–14 in reference to the title "Son of Man."

Spirit of the Reformation Study Bible:

> Daniel saw someone like a man; i.e., someone who was to be compared with a man yet was somehow qualitatively different (v. 14). The expression "son of man" is used 69 times in the Synoptic Gospels and 12 times in John's Gospel to refer to Christ. It is in fact the most common title Jesus used of himself. . . . The One like a man originates in heaven and comes by divine initiative.[3]

3. *Spirit of the Reformation Study Bible* (Grand Rapids: Zondervan, 2003), 1390.

Dennis Johnson:

> As [Stephen] gazed into heaven he saw the glory of God. . . . Moreover, he saw Jesus standing at the right hand of God. . . . The right hand is the position of highest authority in the presence of the Sovereign, and a seated posture implies enthronement [see Psalm 110:1]. In Stephen's vision, however, Jesus was *standing* at God's right hand. . . . In the Sanhedrin's earthly court opponents had (literally) "made false witnesses stand" to speak their slanderous accusations (6:33). . . . Stephen now beheld the heavenly court, where another Witness stood to give testimony, as he had promised: "I tell you, whoever acknowledges me before men, the Son of Man will also acknowledge him before the angels of God" (Luke 12:8).[4]

- Handout question 5: Read the quotation.

8. Refer to the text and read Hebrews 12:15 and the "true woman" statement.
   - Reflect and Pray question 3: Reflect on Hebrews 12:15. Have you seen examples of a woman's bitterness defiling others? Have you seen examples of forgiveness blessing others?

Caution the women about giving names or details. You may want to use hypothetical situations.

9. Reflect and Pray question 5: What is your reaction to the Life-giving Prayer story?
   - This example will help you point to the reality and power of the gospel in our lives.

4. Dennis E. Johnson, *Let's Study Acts* (Carlisle, PA: The Banner of Truth Trust, 2003), 93.

- Be sure the women understand that we may forgive someone but not be able to reconcile. The other person must want reconciliation. It is important for women not to feel guilty if they have attempted reconciliation but it has been rejected.
- How do we know that we have forgiven? If we have given the situation to the Lord, asked Him to cleanse us and give us the grace of forgiveness, and we want the best for the other person, then we have probably forgiven. The memories may flood back at times, and we may see deep roots of bitterness we had not seen before, but when that happens we need to go through the process again. Like the woman in the story, the time will come when we seldom think about it except with gratitude that God has transformed us into forgiven forgivers.
- Handout question 6: Read the quotation.

10. Handout question 7: Discuss how the characteristics of a life-giver are seen when we forgive. Forgiveness gives life to a relationship; unforgiveness takes life from it.

11. Handout question 8: Fill in the blank.

7

FORGIVING: HANDOUT

Acts 7:54–60

1. And he said to all, "If anyone would come after me, let him __________ himself and take up his cross daily and follow me. For whoever would ____________ his life will lose it, but whoever ____________ his life for my sake will save it" (Luke 9:23–24).

2. Create in me a clean heart, O God, and renew a right spirit within me (Ps. 51:10).

3. Responsive reading:

Leader: When Moses came down from Mount Sinai, with the two tablets of the testimony in his hand as he came down from the mountain, Moses did not know that the skin of his face shone because he had been talking with God (Ex. 34:29).

Women: I sought the Lord, and he answered me and delivered me from all my fears. Those who look to him are radiant, and their faces shall never be ashamed (Ps. 34:4–5).

Leader: All who sat in the council saw that [Stephen's] face was like the face of an angel (Acts 6:15).

Women: And we all, with unveiled face, beholding the glory of the Lord, are being transformed into the same image from one degree of glory to another. For this comes from the Lord who is the Spirit (2 Cor. 3:18).

Leader: How do we get a radiant face?

Women: The LORD spoke to Moses, saying, "Speak to Aaron and his sons, saying, Thus you shall bless the people of Israel: you shall say to them,

The LORD bless you and keep you;
the LORD make his face to shine upon you and be gracious to you;
the LORD lift up his countenance upon you and give you peace.

"So shall they put my name upon the people of Israel, and I will bless them" (Num. 6:22–27).

Leader: Let us pray with the psalmist:

All: Make your face shine upon your servant, and teach me your statutes (Ps. 119:135).

The true woman knows that true radiance is reflected radiance. She cannot produce it. She asks the Lord to shine His face upon her so that she might be a forgiver.

4. Themes in Jesus' prayer in John 17:
   God's ______________________
   God's ______________________
   God's ______________________
   God's ______________________
   God's ______________________

5. Dennis Johnson:

> In order to face our adversity with calm trust and treat our enemies with compassion, we too need to see that the Son of Man is at God's right hand, invested with all authority in heaven and on earth. What Stephen experienced in prophetic vision God conveys to us in the sure words of Scripture.[1]

6. Martyn Lloyd-Jones:

> This is Christianity! It not only gives people a different understanding and outlook—it changes their whole spirit and nature. The natural person says, "You hit me, I'll hit you! I must have my rights!" Christians no longer live in that way. They have an entirely different view. There is a new spirit within them, a spirit that can enable them even to love their enemies.[2]

7.

Helper/Life-giver	*Hinderer/Life-taker*
Exodus 18:4 Defends	Attacks
Psalm 10:14 Sees, cares for oppressed	Indifferent, unconcerned for oppressed

1. Johnson, *Let's Study Acts*, 95.
2. Martyn Lloyd-Jones, *Triumphant Christianity: Studies in the Book of Acts, Vol. 5* (Wheaton, IL: Crossway Books, 2006), 245.

Psalm 20:2	Supports	Weakens
Psalm 33:20	Shields, protects	Leaves unprotected
Psalm 70:5	Delivers from distress	Causes distress
Psalm 72:12–14	Rescues poor, weak, needy	Ignores poor, weak, needy
Psalm 86:17	Comforts	Causes discomfort

8. How do we call on God in truth? With __________ for those who hurt us.

The LORD is near to all who call on him,
to all who call on him in truth.
Psalm 145:18

8

HELP: LESSON PLAN

2 Chronicles 20

1. Review
    - Throughout this study we have seen that all the prayers are linked together with overlapping themes and principles. They all tell the one great story of Jesus (you may want to refer to the quotation from Edmund Clowney on the handout for lesson one).
    - This idea is beautifully expressed in the Westminster Larger Catechism.

Handout question 1: Read the question and ask the women to read the answer.

The entire statement is magnificent, but ask the women to underline "by the consent of all the parts, and the scope of the whole, which is to give all glory to God . . ."

Every part of Scripture agrees with every other part. It is all inextricably connected so that the whole gives glory to God by telling His redemption story. This is a captivating concept, and the more we see it the more we understand each part of Scripture. Consider the principles we have identified that help us to know how to call on God in truth. These principles are seen not only in the individual prayers we have studied—they are woven into all the prayers.

- Handout question 1: Fill in the blanks to review the principles.

Watch for these principles as we look at 2 Chronicles 20.

2. Refer to the text and read the first paragraph.
3. The Continuing Story

The biblical narrative is fast-paced and exciting, but it is more than a good read. It is a primer on prayer. Reading these passages will set the context for Jehoshaphat's prayer and for our own prayers. You may want to divide the longer passages into sections.

- 2 Samuel 7:1–17

v. 10: "a house for my name." A house refers to His nearness, His dwelling among us. We have seen that God's name refers to all that He is.

If there is time to read David's response in the rest of the chapter, you will find it instructive.

Handout question 3: Read the quotation.

- 2 Chronicles 6:12–42

Solomon's prayer at the dedication of the temple. Divide this into sections and ask volunteers to read. Briefly discuss with questions such as: What connections do you see to other prayers we have studied? What petitions in this prayer are especially meaningful to you?

- 2 Chronicles 7:1–3

Note the external manifestation of God's glory and the reference to the internal glory of His character (He is good; His steadfast love).

The temple represented God's presence among His people. It was the center of worship and prayer. People who could not go to the temple turned toward Jerusalem when they prayed.

Stanley Gale:

> The temple was God's idea, his initiative. It would symbolize his presence. The temple would serve to convey the majestic transcendence of the holy God, and at the same time communicate the merciful immanence of this God who graciously purposed to dwell among those people he had taken as his very own.[1]

- 2 Chronicles 7:11–16

As we look at Jehoshaphat's prayer we need to put it in this context, but we need to think beyond Jehoshaphat to our own prayers. These passages point to Jesus and our access through Him to the Father.

Handout question 4: Read the quotation and Hebrews 12:1–2.

Refer to John 2:18–21 to see Jesus using the temple imagery to speak of Himself; 1 Corinthians 3:16 to see that the temple

1. Stanley D. Gale, *The Prayer of Jehoshaphat* (Phillipsburg, NJ: P&R Publishing, 2007), 52.

refers to the church; and 1 Corinthians 6:19 to see the reference to individual Christians.

Read Luke 23:44–45. The curtain separated the Holy of Holies from the rest of the temple. Only the high priest was allowed entrance. Through the substitutionary sacrifice of Jesus, the way is open. We have access to God's Presence through Jesus.

Handout question 4: Read Hebrews 4:14, 16 in unison.

This is an amazing invitation, but like Jehoshaphat we don't always avail ourselves of this privilege of access to the throne of God.

4. Reflect and Pray question 1: What are your thoughts about Jehoshaphat's response to His crisis in 2 Chronicles 20 compared with 2 Chronicles 18 and 20:36–37?
   - Jehoshaphat knew God, he knew God's Word, and he knew the story of redemption. This shaped his response and his prayer in chapter 20, but he was careless in the other two episodes. 2 Chronicles 20 is a strong reminder that our first response should be to look to God in prayer.

5. 2 Chronicles 20: Jehoshaphat's Prayer
   - Use the text and the suggestions below.
   - vv. 1–2: What are some enemies that come against women? In addition to the ones mentioned in the text, consider: Boredom—women begin to think their daily responsibilities are routine and meaningless. Spiritual discipline is needed to see all of life, even doing the laundry, as an opportunity to glorify God. Disappointment—our expectations can be an enemy when they cause us to become frustrated.
   - vv. 3–4: What was Jehoshaphat's first instinct? To seek the LORD. Note that this is the name Jehovah,

God's personal name of covenant faithfulness to His people. Jehoshaphat knew God in a personal way.

Handout question 5: Read the quotation.
Read and discuss the "true woman" statement in the text.
Stanley Gale:

> We will be more inclined to seek the Lord properly in extraordinary crisis when we are accustomed to seeking him regularly in the ordinary course of our lives. The better we know God and the more we live in personal communion with him, the more likely and natural it will be for us to turn to him when we are in distress.[2]

Also note that he assembled the people. He did not act independently. Sometimes leaders and parents think they have to act as if they know what to do. Jehoshaphat's leadership is stunning. He asked those under him to pray, and he encouraged them to seek the Lord. It takes resolve to seek the Lord when a rising panic makes us frantically want to seek a solution.

- vv. 5–7

Handout question 6: Read and discuss.

- vv. 8–9

Refer to 2 Chronicles 6:34–35 and emphasize again the symbolism of the temple. Read again the promise in 2 Chronicles 7:15–16. Jehoshaphat was remembering this promise and reminding the people of it.

2. Ibid., 34.

Charles Spurgeon:

> I like to plunge my hand into the promises, and then I find myself able to grasp with a grip of determination the mighty faithfulness of God.[3]

- vv. 10–12

What is your reaction to Jehoshaphat's admission that he was powerless and ignorant? There is a sense of relief when we realize that we do not know what to do and that our responsibility is to fix our eyes on Jesus.

- vv. 13–17

Use the text to discuss this section. Use questions such as: How does gathering with others and listening to God's Word as it is read and taught help us face our crises? What are your thoughts about v. 17?

- vv. 18–19

Recap the progression we see:

(1) Seek the Lord.
(2) Remember His power, plan, and eternal purpose.
(3) Remember His presence with us.
(4) Acknowledge our helplessness and petition Him to deal with the crisis.

3. C. H. Spurgeon, *The Treasury of the Bible, Old Testament, Vol. 2, I Chronicles to Psalm CXI* (Grand Rapids: Zondervan, 1962), 75.

(5) Wait on Him in faith and stay in His Word.
(6) Worship and thank Him for what He will do.

When we seek the Lord in this way, courage and commitment grow in our hearts. This is what we see in verses 20–21.

- vv. 20–30

Use the Scriptures and the text to recount this thrilling story.

6. Handout question 7: Fill in the blank.
7. Reflect and Pray question 2: What is most helpful to you about 2 Chronicles 20? Share answers to this question.
8. Reflect and Pray question 3: Personalize 2 Chronicles 7:14–16 and write it in your own words. Ask volunteers to read what they wrote.

8

HELP: HANDOUT

2 Chronicles 20

1. Westminster Larger Catechism

   Q. 4. How doth it appear that the scriptures are the word of God?
   A. The scriptures manifest themselves to be the word of God, by their majesty and purity; by the consent of all the parts, and the scope of the whole, which is to give all glory to God; by their light and power to convince and convert sinners, to comfort and build up believers unto salvation: but the Spirit of God bearing witness by and with the scriptures in the heart of man, is alone able fully to persuade it that they are the very word of God.

2. How do we call on God in truth?
   Genesis 1–3: With ____________________ for our redemption.
   John 17:1–5: Pray for His ______________.
   Pray according to His eternal __________ and __________.

John 17:6–19: Approach Him as our ____________.
Pray in Jesus' ________________.
Praying according to His ______________.
John 17:20–26: With an __________ perspective, seeing myself united in love to Christ and to the great company of the redeemed in all ages.
Exodus 32–34: Appeal on the basis of His _________.
Psalm 51: With a ____________ and believing heart.
Acts 7:54–60: With ______________ for those who hurt us.

3. 2 Samuel 7:1–17

ESV Study Bible note on 2 Samuel 7:

This chapter, with its messianic promise, is a key passage in the history of salvation. The Lord promises to make one family, that of David, the representative of his people forever. Verses 8–17 are often described as the "Davidic covenant," . . . David expresses his desire to build a house for the Lord. But the Lord does not approve, and instead states on his own initiative that he will establish David's house (i.e., dynasty) eternally. . . . This points to Solomon, who would "sit on the throne of Israel" and build "the house for the name of the LORD" (1 Kings 8:20), and eventually to Jesus, the Messiah who would sit on the throne eternally, thus establishing David's throne forever.[1]

4. Charles Spurgeon:

We have no sacred spot now, beloved friends, towards which we turn when we pray. . . . Yet we have a Temple . . . we

1. *English Standard Version Study Bible* (Wheaton, IL: Crossway Bibles, 2008), 554.

have an altar. . . . Our Temple is the person of the Lord Jesus Christ. . . . When we pray, we turn our faces toward Him. . . . yet is He infinitely more precious and far greater than the temple; and whosoever, whatsoever his trouble shall be, shall pray unto God with his face towards Jesus, looking to the matchless wounds by which He has redeemed us, or the glorified person in which He represents us, and makes intercession for us before the throne of God on high, he shall be helped, he shall be forgiven, whatever his trouble or whatever his sin.[2]

Therefore, since we are surrounded by so great a cloud of witnesses, let us also lay aside every weight, and sin which clings so closely, and let us run with endurance the race that is set before us, looking to Jesus, the founder and perfecter of our faith. (Heb. 12:1–2)

Since then we have a great high priest who has passed through the heavens, Jesus, the Son of God, let us hold fast our confession. . . . Let us then with confidence draw near to the throne of grace, that we may receive mercy and find grace to help in time of need. (Heb. 4:14, 16)

5. Stanley Gale:

Three times in verses 3 and 4 we read of Jehoshaphat and the people seeking the Lord. . . . Seeking him does not involve searching for him. Seeking him involves turning to him, focusing our gaze, seeing beyond the storm to behold him who reigns. The obstacle is not God, but us in our attentiveness to him.[3]

2. Spurgeon, *The Treasury of the Bible*, 54.
3. Gale, *The Prayer of Jehoshaphat*, 31.

> Seek the LORD while he may be found; call upon him while he is near. (Isa. 55:6)

6. Stanley Gale:

> In times of crisis, we do want to rush to prayer but not rush to petition. Reflecting is to precede requesting. King Jehoshaphat nestled himself in the arms of God with each name he invoked. In those times of distress in our lives, we want to remind ourselves of the God we seek and what right of access we have. It is here that our prayer is infused with expectation.[4]

7. How do we call on God in truth? In ____________ and in ______________.

4. Ibid.

The LORD is near to all who call on him,

to all who call on him in truth.

Psalm 145:18

9

KNOWLEDGE: LESSON PLAN

Ephesians 1:15–23

1. Review
   - In each of the prayers we have studied, the person was facing a specific situation. What is something you learned from them that is shaping your own prayers as you face the circumstances of your life? How are they helping you to call on God in truth? Jesus' prayer in John 17? Moses' petitions in Exodus 32–34? David's prayer in Psalm 51? Stephen's prayer in Acts 7. Jehoshaphat's prayer in 2 Chronicles 20?

With Paul's prayers in Ephesians it is as if he, too, had studied these prayers. Here we see how someone who knows the principles of calling on God in truth lives and prays. These principles affect not only our prayers; they affect our living.

2. Refer to the text and discuss the first two paragraphs and the quotation from James Boice. Emphasize that

what we see in Paul's prayers in Ephesians is a life perspective, a world- and life-view, that equips us to live for God's glory.

- This is the same idea that we saw in the phrases from the Westminster Larger Catechism in reference to God's Word: "the consent of all the parts, and the scope of the whole, which is to give all glory to God" (see handout for lesson eight).

All of the parts of God's Word, and the scope of the whole of His Word, give glory to God. In Ephesians 1 we see that all of the parts of our lives work together to accomplish the same purpose—to glorify Him.

- Handout question 1: Read the outline and quotation.
- As you work through the passage, use the text and the material below. After discussing each section ask whether there are other reactions or questions.

3. vv. 1–14
   - Ask: What are the themes we saw in John 17? God's glory, people, nearness, calling, and love. Note these themes as we read this passage.
   - We considered these verses in lesson one. This takes us back to before the beginning to see what the natural mind cannot see. Here we are told about the great reality of the transcendent God coming near. This truth will determine our perspective of life and of prayer.
   - Handout question 2: Fill in the blanks—chose, redeems, guarantees, God's glory, sovereign. God's nearness is because of His sovereign initiative. He comes to us.

- Refer to Acts 17:26–28 in the text.

Reflect and Pray question 1: How does knowing that God determined the time in history and the place on the planet where you would live change your perspective about the events and relationships in your life?

Read the "true woman" statement on the handout. This prayer focuses us on God's glory rather than on ourselves. This is a practical help in praying for others: Father, give her strength to glorify you in her relationship with . . . , or as she faces . . .

- Suggestion: Have a time of prayer and ask the women to use vv. 1–14 to form their praise, and Acts 17:26–28 to shape their petition about their circumstances and relationships.

4. vv. 15–16
    - Handout question 3: Fill in the blanks—redemption, faith, love. He prays for those that vv. 3–14 refer to, so they are the ones God gave to Jesus.
    - Why does he give thanks *for* them rather than *to* them? He acknowledges that their faith and love are gifts of God's grace.
    - Paul says that he does not cease to pray for them. This is a prayer for spiritual maturity, which is a process, so we need to persevere in prayer.

5. v. 17
    - Handout question 4: Fill in the blanks—know.
    - The essence of Paul's prayer for them is that they will know Christ.

6. v. 18–20
   - Handout question 5: Discuss the Scriptures and quotation.

Note the "I wills" in Ezekiel 37—God's sovereign initiative. Emphasize the work of the Holy Spirit in our spiritual growth.

Charles Spurgeon:

> How should the body of a man without any means be borne upward into the air? . . . So the Christian's rising above the world, His breathing another atmosphere, is clean contrary to nature. How would you wonder if you saw a man suddenly rise up into the sky? Wonder more when you see a Christian rise above temptation, worldliness, and sin; when you discover him forsaking those things which once were his delight, and mounting towards heaven.[1]

Ask: What is the difference in praying for someone's behavior to change and praying that God will open the eyes of his/her heart to know Him better?

This is an important petition whenever we read God's Word or prepare our hearts for worship.

Handout question 6: Use the text to fill in the blanks and to discuss this section. After discussing each one, ask: How does knowing this truth help us to know God better and to mature in faith?

(1) Called. Our *calling* to glorify God was one of the themes we identified in John 17. Ephesians 1:1–14 expounds on this calling. It is rooted in eternity past (v. 4). It is present (v. 4)—we are called to be holy and blameless. It is future (vv. 11–14). Because of the Triune God's sovereign grace we can fulfill our calling to glorify Him.

1. C. H. Spurgeon, *The Treasury of the Bible, New Testament, Vol. Three* (Grand Rapids: Zondervan Publishing House, 1962), 356.

(2) Inheritance. The truth that we belong to Him, not because of anything in us but because of His sovereign love, is essential for spiritual maturity.

ESV Study Bible:

The "inheritance" here is not the Christian's inheritance but his (God's). This indicates how precious his people are to God. They are, so to speak, what he looks forward to enjoying forever.[2]

What was Jesus' final petition in John 17:24? He wants us to be with Him.

(3) Power. It is staggering to think that we have the same power that raised Jesus from the dead. We have His Holy Spirit living in us. This is the power that will enable us to live out our calling to glorify Him in a fallen world. This is the power that will keep us to the end and take us to heaven.

Reflect and Pray question 3: What are your thoughts about having the same power that raised Jesus from the dead available to empower you to know and serve Him? Emphasize that this is the power than enables us to be life-givers. You may want to refer to the life-giver/life-taker chart (handout lesson one and seven).

- Handout question 6: Read the quotation from Spurgeon.

7. vv. 21–22
   - Jesus is ruling and reigning over heaven and earth for the sake of His church. The promise to David (2 Samuel 7:11–16) has been kept.

2. *English Standard Version Study Bible* (Wheaton, IL: Crossway Bibles, 2008), 2263.

Refer to vv. 9–12. Because Jesus was victorious over sin and death, the "plan for the fullness of time, to unite all things in him," is being carried out. He is working "all things according to the counsel of His will" in order that we might praise His glorious grace. Nothing is random; nothing is wasted.

Refer again to the phrases from the Westminster Larger Catechism, "the consent of all the parts, and the scope of the whole, which is to give all glory to God."

How does He refer to the church in v. 23? Adam spoke of Eve as "bone of my bones and flesh of my flesh" (Genesis 2:23). We are the body of Christ, the bride of Christ.

Handout question 7: Read the quotation.

8. Reflect and Pray question 2: Ask volunteers to read their prayers based on this passage.

9. Handout question 8: Fill in the blank.
    - Charles Spurgeon:

> To trust Christ, to depend upon his power and faithfulness, is such a childlike act that one sees no extraordinary difficulty in it. Yet . . . to bring down the pride of man, to subjugate his will and to captivate his passions, so that he shall cheerfully accept that which God presents to him in the person of Christ Jesus, is a labour worthy of a God. . . . The bringing of a soul to simple faith in Jesus, and the maintenance of that soul in the life of faith, displays an exercise of omnipotence such as God alone could put forth. . . . It is not only the first act of conversion which displays divine power, but the whole of the Christian's career, until he comes to perfection.[3]

3. Spurgeon, *The Treasury of the Bible*, 354–55.

9

KNOWLEDGE: HANDOUT

Ephesians 1:15–23

1. Outline of Ephesians 1
   vv. 1–18: Doxology to the Trinity for planning and accomplishing redemption
   vv. 19–23: Prayer that God will complete this redemption in His people as they grow in the knowledge of Him

John Stott:

> He begins with a great benediction (1:3–14) and continues with a great intercession (1:15–23). Ephesians 1 is, in fact, divided into these two sections. First, he blesses God for having blessed us in Christ; then he prays that God will open our eyes to grasp the fullness of this blessing. . . . If we keep together praise and prayer, benediction and petition, we are unlikely to lose our spiritual equilibrium.[1]

1. John R. W. Stott, *The Message of Ephesians* (Downers Grove, IL: InterVarsity Press, 1979), 51–52.

2. Ephesians 1:3–14
   vv. 3–6: The Father ________________ us before creation.
   vv. 7–12: The Son ____________________ us.
   vv. 13–14: The Spirit _________________ our inheritance.
   vv. 6, 12, 13: The purpose __________________________.
   This shows us God's _________________________ grace.

The true woman knows that God has sovereignly determined her time and place. Her prayer is:
• How can I glorify you in this relationship/situation?

3. vv. 15–16
   - Paul's reason for this prayer: The __________________ planned, accomplished, and applied by the triune God. His prayer is based on what God has done.
   - What is the evidence of God's work in the Ephesians? Their ________ in Jesus and __________ for each other.

4. v. 17
   - What is Paul's petition? That they will __________ God.
   - What did Jesus say in John 17:3? "And this is eternal life, that they ________ you the only true God, and Jesus Christ whom you have sent."
   - What did Moses pray in Exodus 33:13? "Now therefore, if I have found favor in your sight, please show me now your ways, that I may _______ you."

5. vv. 18–25: Why does he pray that God will open the eyes of their hearts?

The natural person does not accept the things of the Spirit of God, for they are folly to him, and he is not able to understand them because they are spiritually discerned. (I Cor. 2:14)

I will sprinkle clean water on you, and you shall be clean from all your uncleannesses, and from all your idols I will cleanse you. And I will give you a new heart, and a new spirit I will put within you. And I will remove the heart of stone from your flesh and give you a heart of flesh. And I will put my Spirit within you, and cause you to walk in my statutes and be careful to obey my rules. (Ezek. 37:25–27)

When the Spirit of truth comes, he will guide you into all the truth. (John 16:13)

R. C. Sproul:

The heart in New Testament terms refers to the central disposition, inclination, bent, or proclivity of the human soul. . . . The whole Christian life involves an unfolding and enlarging of the heart's openness to the things of God. . . . Sin clouds my thinking, my will, my desires, my affections. There will always be parts of me that need to be opened more and more to let the fullness of God's truth dwell in me.[2]

6. What are the three truths that Paul prays they will know?
   (1) The hope to which He has __________ us.
   (2) We are His ________________________.
   (3) The greatness of His _____________ in us.

2. R. C. Sproul, *The Purpose of God, An Exposition of Ephesians* (Fearn, Scotland: Christian Focus Publications, 1994), 39–40.

Charles Spurgeon:

> Why does God put forth as much power towards every Christian as He did in His beloved Son? Well, my brethren, I believe the reason is not only that the same power was required, and that by this means He getteth great glory, but the reason is this—*union.* There must be the same divine power in the member that there is in the Head, or else where is the union? If we are one with Christ, members of His body, of His flesh, and of His bones, there must be a likeness.[3]

7. Charles Spurgeon:

> He is a good husband. He will enjoy nothing without His spouse. When she was poor, He became poor for her sake; when she was despised, He was spit upon too; and now that He is in heaven, He must have her there. If He sits on a throne, she must have a throne too; if He has fullness of joy, and honour, and glory for ever—then so must she. He will not be in heaven, and leave her behind; and He will not enjoy a single privilege of heaven, without her being a sharer with Him.[4]

8. How do we call on God in truth? Continually ask Him to open the eyes of our heart that we might __________ Him better.

3. Spurgeon, *The Treasury of the Bible*, 367.
4. Ibid., 358.

The LORD is near to all who call on him,

to all who call on him in truth.

Psalm 145:18

10

POWER: LESSON PLAN

Ephesians 3:14–21

1. Review
   - What was the essence of Paul's prayer in Ephesians 1? That we would know Christ.
   - What are the three great truths that Paul prays we will know so that we will know Christ better? The hope to which He has called us. We are His inheritance. The greatness of His power in us.
   - How does he describe this power? It is the same power that raised Jesus from the dead. It is the power of the Holy Spirit.
   - In Ephesians 3 he continues his prayer, and the essence of this prayer is that we will have power.
   - How did he begin his prayer in Ephesians 1:15? For this reason.
     How does he begin chapter 3? For this reason.
     How does he begin his prayer in 3:14? For this reason.
     What is the reason? The reason includes everything he has said in his letter about God's sovereign grace and love

for His people, the ones He gave to Jesus, His church. The basis of his prayer is God's plan and purpose.

- Handout question 1: Ask volunteers to read the verses to see the theme of the church in Ephesians.

2. Use the text and the following information. Begin by reading vv. 14–21.

3. vv. 14–15
   - Paul kneels in humility and yet he recognizes God as the Father of His people. This familial relationship with the God of heaven and earth is what Jesus taught in John 17 when He addressed God as Father, and we will see in the Lord's Prayer that He teaches us to do the same. These words emphasize our oneness with God and with one another.

Our relationship with Him gives us our individual and corporate identities. In Exodus 33:16 Moses prayed: "Is it not in your going with us, so that we are distinct, I and your people, from every other people on the face of the earth?" It is the presence of God that distinguishes and unites us.

- Refer to the text and read the quotation from Spurgeon from the funeral of a woman in his church. How would you describe this woman? She was a true woman, a life-giver.
- Handout question 2: Fill in the blanks—knowledge, power.

Why do you think he continues to emphasize our need for God's power? Because we are powerless to come near or stay near to Christ. We are totally dependent on the power of the gospel, and Paul is not ashamed of that power (Rom. 1:16).

4. vv. 16–17
    - Handout question 2: Fill in the blank (1)—change.
    - This is an amazing concept. Summarize the text and use the following questions:

      Reflect and Pray question 1: What are some things you need strength to change?

      You may want to make this generic and ask: What are things we need strength to change?

      Ideas: You may want to refer to the characteristics of God in Exodus 34:6–7 and ask: What is the opposite of each one?

This is what we are naturally. We need power to change. You may want to use Galatians 5:16–26 and see a similar contrast. We need God's power to change from being self-centered to God-centered. We need His power to repent and turn from our idols, to resist temptation, to make the right moral choices, to forgive those who hurt us, to serve without resentment, to suffer without frustration, to age without bitterness.

Do you find it discouraging or encouraging to admit your need for God's power to change?

How does this help you in praying for others?

Often we expect others to change their attitudes when they are as powerless as we are. The hope of the gospel is the power of the Holy Spirit in us to produce His fruit in us.

- Handout question 2: Read the quotation from Ligon Duncan.

5. vv. 17–19
    - Handout question 2: Fill in the blank (2)—love.
    - Summarize the text. Also use Reflect and Pray questions 2 and 3.
    - Note the progression: As Christ dwells in us, the power of His nearness transforms specific spaces in our hearts. We increasingly reflect the glory of His character by loving others. As this happens, we know more of His limitless love for us. We are transformed from life-takers to life-givers. This reminds us of Exodus 34:10: "Before all your people I will do marvels. . . . It is an awesome thing that I will do with you."
    - Handout question 2: Read the quotations from Ligon Duncan and John Stott.
    - Refer to v. 19, "filled with all the fullness of God." Use the following illustration:

James Boice:

When Napoleon's armies opened a prison that had been used by the Spanish Inquisition they found the remains of a prisoner who had been incarcerated for his faith. The dungeon was underground. The body had long since decayed. Only a chain fastened around an anklebone cried out his confinement. But this prisoner, long since dead, had left a witness. On the wall of his small, dismal cell this faithful soldier of Christ had scratched a rough cross with four words surrounding it in Spanish. Above the cross was the Spanish word for "height." Below it was the word for "depth." To the left the word "width." To the right, the word "length." Clearly this prisoner wanted to testify to the surpassing greatness of the love of Christ, perceived even in his suffering.[1]

Handout question 3: Refer to the cross and ask the women to write "height" at the top; at the bottom write "depth"; on one side write "width"; on the other side write "length." Read the quotation from John Stott.

6. vv. 20–22
    - Summarize the text and the following quotations.
    - James Boice:

> I do not know how God is going to do that, and I will tell you something interesting: even though he talks about it, I do not think Paul understood it either. . . . When Paul says "we" he includes himself. He is saying that even he, the great apostle, cannot fully understand or even imagine all that God is going to do for us. But Paul does know that God can do it. . . . My mind stops at that, and I think that is where Paul's mind stopped too. . . . It remains only to say, as Paul does, "to Him be glory in the church and in Christ Jesus throughout all generations, for ever and ever! Amen."[2]

- Charles Spurgeon:

> Our boldest prayer is not the boundary of what He is able to bestow.[3]

1. James Montgomery Boice, *Ephesians, An Expositional Commentary* (Grand Rapids: Baker Books, 1998), 111.
2. Ibid., 112.
3. C. H. Spurgeon, *The Treasury of the New Testament, Vol. 3* (Grand Rapids: Zondervan Publishing House, 1962), 419.

- D. A. Carson:

> The ultimate purpose of Paul's prayer is that there be glory to God, in the church and in Christ Jesus. . . . We may have improved a little on the quality of what we ask for, but the deeper question is this: Do we bring these petitions before God both with a proximate goal (that we might receive what we ask for) and with an ultimate goal—that God might be glorified? For that, surely, is the deepest test: Has God become so central to all our thought and pursuits, and thus to our praying, that we cannot easily imagine asking for anything without consciously longing that the answer bring glory to God.[4]

- Handout question 4: Read the quotation from Charles Spurgeon.

7. Ask: How would you summarize this prayer? How does it help you to pray for yourself and others?
8. Handout question 5: Fill in the blanks.
9. Refer to the Life-giving Prayer section in the text and discuss these ideas. Ask women for other ideas to share.

4. D. A. Carson, *A Call to Spiritual Reformation* (Grand Rapids: Baker Academic, 1992), 203.

10

POWER: HANDOUT

Ephesians 3:14–21

1. Do we have the kind of vision of the church that Paul had? Remember, there were no influential megachurches. There were only small house churches, yet Paul saw beyond the visible to the invisible realities. As we understand the cosmic transcendent realities of the church, our perspective of our local church and the privilege of being a part of it will be transformed. Read the following verses from Ephesians to see Paul's emphasis on the church.
   - 1:22
   - 2:18–22
   - 3:6
   - 3:7–11
   - 4:11–13
   - 4:15–16
   - 5:22–24

- 5:25–27
- 5:29–32

2. In Ephesians 1, Paul prays that we will have ____________.

   In chapter 3 he prays that we will have ________________.

   He divides this petition into two parts:

   (1) Power to ________________.

Ligon Duncan:

> To be indwelt by Christ means that our hearts, the very essence of our minds, wills, and affections, the core of our inner being, becomes a suitable habitation for Christ. . . . Paul tells us that the Holy Spirit does a work of interior decoration in us so that . . . people begin to recognize that our desires and priorities look like Christ.[1]

   (2) Power to ________________.

Ligon Duncan:

> The bride of Christ knows that she is called to do things she does not have the strength to do, and she knows that the Holy Spirit supplies that strength. So if we are going to look like the bride of Christ, we must live in dependence upon the spiritual strength that only God can supply. One way this will manifest itself is prayer. Prayer itself is an act of continual confession that we do not have what we need in ourselves to live and minister as we are called to do and that we look to our heavenly Father to supply our need.[2]

1. Ligon Duncan and Susan Hunt, *Women's Ministry in the Local Church* (Wheaton, IL: Crossway Books, 2006), 149.
2. Ibid., 147.

John Stott:

> In the new and reconciled humanity which Christ is creating love is the pre-eminent virtue. The new humanity is God's family, whose members are brothers and sisters, who love their Father and love each other. Or should do. They need the power of the Spirit's might and of Christ's indwelling to enable them to love each other.[3]

3. "[I pray that you] may have strength to comprehend with all the saints what is the breadth and length and height and depth, and to know the love of Christ that surpasses knowledge, that you may be filled with all the fullness of God" (Eph. 3:18–19).

John Stott:

> The love of Christ is "broad" enough to encompass all mankind . . . "long" enough to last for eternity, "deep" enough to reach the most degraded sinner, and "high" enough to exalt him to heaven. . . . Ancient commentators . . . saw these dimensions illustrated on the cross. For its upright pole reached down into the earth and

3. John R. W. Stott, *The Message of Ephesians* (Downers Grove, IL: InterVarsity Press, 1979), 136.

pointed up to heaven, while its crossbar carried the arms of Jesus, stretched out as if to invite and welcome the whole world.[4]

4. To him be glory in the church and in Christ Jesus throughout all generations, forever and ever. Amen (Eph. 3:21).

Charles Spurgeon:

If unto Him there should be glory in the Church throughout all ages, then, to Him should there be glory in this Church at this present moment. O Lord, help us to render it unto Thee.[5]

5. How do we call on God in prayer? Ask for power to be filled with the __________ of God that He might be ____________ in His church.

4. Ibid., 137.
5. Spurgeon, *The Treasury of the New Testament*, 417.

The LORD is near to all who call on him,

to all who call on him in truth.

Psalm 145:18

11

LIFE: LESSON PLAN

1 Samuel 1:1–2:10

1. Review
   - In lesson one, we learned about the true woman.

Handout question 1: Fill in the blanks—glory, Word, happiness, herself.

Refer to the chart. In 1 Samuel we see that Hannah was a life-giver in her relationships.

   - Hannah's relationships provide a good review of the true woman/life-giver concept. Use the text and the information below.

2. 1 Samuel 1:1–3
   - Refer to the text and summarize the opening paragraphs.
   - Ralph Klein:

> The motif of a barren wife who is given a child by Yahweh and whose child plays an important role is quite frequent in the OT. . . .

The effect of these moving stories is to underscore the importance of the son who is born and to indicate the fact that he is God's gift.[1]

- Robert Bergen:

In this passage [referring to the Lord closing Hannah's womb, v. 5] Israelite faith expresses its supreme paradox and boldest affirmation—the Lord may create social and natural tragedies in order to accomplish his purposes that far outweigh the calamity. [2]

- You may want to refer to Joshua 18:1 to explain why they went to Shiloh.

3. Discuss each of Hannah's relationships in 1 Samuel: her rival (vv. 4–7), her husband (vv. 8–9), her pastor (vv. 9–18).
   - Summarize the text and use the following questions to discuss each relationship:
     What do you learn from Hannah's relationship with him/her?
     What helper/life-giver characteristic do you see Hannah demonstrate in this relationship?
     Describe how you think this relationship would look if Hannah had been a new woman.

Refer to Ephesians 3:14–21. What do you think Hannah had to pray for power to do?

If you were in a similar relationship, what other prayer that we have studied would be helpful to you?

1. Ralph W. Klein, *Word Biblical Commentary, 1 Samuel* (Waco, TX: Word Books, 1983), 4.

2. Robert D. Bergen, *1, 2 Samuel: The New American Commentary, An Exegetical and Theological Exposition of Holy Scripture* (Broadman & Holman Publishers, 1996), 63.

Handout question 2: Read and discuss.

4. vv. 19–28
   - v. 19 says, "The Lord remembered." Robert Bergen: "'Remembered' is a soteriological verb when used with the Lord as the subject and suggests the initiation of a major new activity by the covenant-making God."[3]
   - Various meanings of the name Samuel are suggested: heard of God, he who is from God. The idea is: gift of God.
   - Leaving Samuel at the temple was an act of obedience and an act of faith. Eli's sons were engaging in vile behavior (2:27–36). Hannah trusted God's sovereignty. This was God's plan and purpose for Samuel, so it was the safest place in the world for him to be. The quietness and trust of Hannah's heart is a testimony to every Christian mother.
   - Summarize the text. Refer to the section about a husband trusting his heart to his wife. Refer to the life-giver/life-taker chart. How does each side of this chart build or destroy trust?
   - Hannah is not simply an example to follow. Being a life-giver means a change of heart, not a self-effort change in behavior. Hannah's story is an example of the power of the gospel enabling a woman to *be* and *do* "more abundantly than all that we ask or think, according to the power at work within us" for the glory of God throughout all generations (Eph. 3:20–21).

3. Ibid., 70.

5. vv. 10–11
   - In Hannah's petition she addresses God as LORD of hosts.

Robert Bergen:

Her pain had made her a theologian—no character in Scripture prior to Hannah had ever used this term to address the Lord. In her prayer she implicitly recognized that the Lord alone is the giver of life. She also understood that the proper position of a believer in relation to the Lord is that of absolute subjection; three times she referred to herself as "your servant," a term used elsewhere to describe a female household slave. Furthermore, she recognized that a relationship with the Lord involves giving, not just taking. She made a vow—an act without parallel for women elsewhere in Hebrew narrative but conditionally permissible for a married woman (cf. Num. 30:6–8)—to "give [him] to the LORD for all the days of his life."[4]

6. 2 Samuel 2:1–10
   - Use the text and the following to work through this magnificent prayer.

Spirit of the Reformation Study Bible:

Hannah accompanied the fulfillment of her vow with a jubilant song of thanksgiving. Focusing in hymnic fashion on the Lord's judgment of the proud and his grace to the humble, Hannah anticipated dominant themes throughout 1 and 2 Samuel. These themes are reiterated

4. Ibid., 68.

in David's own song of thanksgiving near the end of 2 Samuel (chap. 22). Thus the two songs together provide a poetic frame for 1 and 2 Samuel. Moreover, these themes extend far beyond the book of Samuel, reaching all the way to the New Testament.[5]

- Handout question 3: Fill in the blank—anointed—and read the explanations.
- Refer to the text and read the "true woman" statement.
- Reflect and Pray question 2: What did you learn from Hannah's prayers? How did she call on God in truth? Refer to the principles that have been identified in previous prayers.

7. Refer to the text and summarize the section: Hannah's Legacy
   - Hannah was a Titus 2 woman in Mary's life. So was Elizabeth. In Luke 1:39–45 we read that after Mary received word that she would be the mother of the Messiah, she hurried to Elizabeth's home. Elizabeth welcomed, affirmed, and encouraged Mary, and Mary sang a song of praise to the Lord. It is noteworthy that Mary did not sing this song of praise until she had been loved and encouraged by an older woman. This is Titus 2 discipleship.

Handout question 4
Read the quotation and then read Luke 1:46–55 responsively.

5. *Spirit of the Reformation Study Bible* (Grand Rapids: Zondervan, 2003), 396.

- Reflect and Pray question 3: Read Mary's Magnificat in Luke 1:46–55 and list similarities in Hannah's prayer in 1 Samuel 2:1–10.

Spirit of the Reformation Study Bible:

Mary's song of praise (the Magnificat) reflects Hannah's song; e.g., both Hannah's and Mary's songs open with jubilation over the Lord's deliverance (v. 1; Lk 1:46–48), both extol the Lord's uniqueness and holiness (v. 2; Lk 1:49–50), both condemn proud boasting (v. 3; Lk 1:51), both point to reversals of human fortune as the result of interventions by the sovereign Lord (vv. 4–8; Lk 1:52–53) and both express the Lord's faithful care for his own (v. 9; Lk 1:54–55).[6]

8. Handout question 5: Fill in the blanks.

9. Refer to the Life-giving Prayer story in the text and ask for reactions. Others may have similar stories.

6. Ibid.

11

LIFE: HANDOUT

1 Samuel 1:1–2:10

1. The true woman:
   - Her purpose is God's __________________.
   - Her authority is God's __________________.

   The new woman:
   - Her purpose is her ________________________.
   - Her authority is ___________________________.

The True Woman	***The New Woman***
Helper/Life-giver	*Hinderer/Life-taker*
Exodus 18:4 Defends	Attacks
Psalm 10:14 Sees, cares for oppressed	Indifferent, unconcerned for oppressed
Psalm 20:2 Supports	Weakens
Psalm 33:20 Shields, protects	Leaves unprotected
Psalm 70:5 Delivers from distress	Causes distress
Psalm 72:12–14 Pities the poor, weak, needy	Ignores poor, weak, needy
Psalm 86:17 Comforts	Causes discomfort

2. A true woman's questions:
   How do I glorify God in this relationship?
   What will it mean to submit this relationship to the authority of God's Word?

3. How did Hannah conclude her prayer in 2 Samuel 10? By referring to the "horn of his ______________."

Horn refers to strength.
Spirit of the Reformation Study Bible:

It is from the Hebrew word for "anointed" that we derive the term "Messiah" and from the Greek word for "anointed" that we derive "Christ." Hannah's celebration culminated in thoughts of the king, much as Christians find their hope in the exaltation of Christ.[1]

4. Hannah's Prayer/Mary's Prayer

Robert Bergen:

The close parallels between Hannah's Prayer and Mary's Song (Luke 1:46–55) suggest that the first-century Christian community considered the entire passage, and especially the phrases "his king" and "his anointed," to be prophetic references to Jesus Christ and his ministry.[2]

The Magnificat (Luke 1:46–55)

Leader: And Mary said, "My soul magnifies the Lord, and my spirit rejoices in God my Savior, for he has looked on the

1. Ibid., 397.
2. Bergen, *1, 2 Samuel*, 77.

humble estate of his servant. For behold, from now on all generations will call me blessed; for he who is mighty has done great things for me, and holy is his name.

Women: And his mercy is for those who fear him from generation to generation.

Leader: He has shown strength with his arm; he has scattered the proud in the thoughts of their hearts;

Women: He has brought down the mighty from their thrones and exalted those of humble estate;

Leader: He has filled the hungry with good things, and the rich he has sent empty away.

Women: He has helped his servant Israel, in remembrance of his mercy, as he spoke to our fathers, to Abraham and to his offspring forever."

5. How do we call on God in truth? Humbly ___________ to His ___________.

The LORD is near to all who call on him,

to all who call on him in truth.

Psalm 145:18

12

KINGDOM: LESSON PLAN

MATTHEW 6:9–13

1. Review
   - What were the themes we saw in John 17? God's glory, God's people, God's nearness, God's calling, God's love. These themes are woven into every prayer we have studied, and we see them in the Lord's Prayer.
   - What are the principles we have identified that answer the question: How do we call on God in truth?
     1. (Genesis 1–3) Pray with gratitude for our redemption.
     2. (John 17) Pray for His glory; pray according to His eternal plan and purpose.
     3. (John 17) Approach Him as our Father; pray in Jesus' name; pray according to His Word.
     4. (John 17) Pray with an eternal perspective, seeing myself united in love to Christ and to the great company of the redeemed in all ages.
     5. (Moses) Appeal on the basis of His character.
     6. (David) Pray with a repentant and believing heart.
     7. (Stephen) Ask with mercy for those who hurt us.

8. (Jehoshaphat) Pray in quietness and in trust.
9. (Ephesians 1) Ask Him continually to open the eyes of our hearts that we might know Him better.
10. (Ephesians 3) Ask for power to be filled with the fullness of God that He might be glorified in His church.
11. (Hannah) Humbly submit to His sovereignty.

Emphasize that this is not an exhaustive list. Neither is it a formula. These are simply principles to guide us in prayer. These principles do not stand alone. They all work together to equip us to glorify God in our prayers.

2. Refer to the text and summarize the opening paragraph.

3. The kingdom of God
   - Matthew 6:9–11 is part of the Sermon on the Mount (chaps. 5–7).

Spirit of the Reformation Study Bible:

> The kingdom of God . . . undergirds the teaching of the entire Bible. The Scriptures reveal God using a number of metaphors, but the primary imagery that Biblical writers used for God was that of a divine king. . . . [Matthew] 5–7 present more information on the ethical standards of God's sovereign reign than any other text. . . . The kingdom Jesus was talking about was the kingdom he inaugurated during his earthly ministry, and the ethics of that kingdom were immediately applicable to his disciples. Jesus also proclaimed the kingdom's transforming power, which enables believers to live according to kingdom ethics.[1]

1. *Spirit of the Reformation Study Bible* (Grand Rapids: Zondervan, 2003), 1550.

Prayer is an essential element of kingdom life. The kingdom idea infuses our prayers with vision and energy.

Charles Dunahoo:

> If we have the right kingdom perspective, then we will know there is no area of life about which God is not concerned and over which he is not the sovereign Lord. The apostle Paul says, "So, whether you eat or drink, or whatever you do, do all to the glory of God" (1 Cor. 10:31). . . . In using the idea of the kingdom the Bible seeks to underscore the kingship of Jesus Christ, in terms of both the total creational *realm* over which he is sovereign and his *reign* over all dimensions of his subjects' lives. . . . Understanding the all-inclusiveness of the kingdom will remind us that everything we do is a religious activity and is to be done to the glory of God. . . . By looking at the church, people should see more clearly than in any other place what the kingdom of God is like because it is the heart of the kingdom.[2]

4. Handout question 1: The text gives some introductory quotations about this prayer. Read these additional quotations.

5. Read Matthew 6:1–13.
   - Some translations do not include the ending, "For yours is the kingdom and the power and the glory forever. Amen." Usually there is a note that explains that this is included only in some later manuscripts of Matthew.
   - Reflect and Pray question 1: What does Jesus warn against in Matthew 6:5–8? By contrast, what is the focus in verses 9–13?

2. Charles H. Dunahoo, *Making Kingdom Disciples* (Phillipsburg, NJ.: P&R Publishing, 2005), 40–43, 47.

Handout question 2: Fill in the blanks—self, God.

This contrast is instructive. Calling on God in truth means that we focus on Him, His will, and His glory.

6. Use the text, handout questions 3–10, and the material below to work through this prayer. The text uses the Westminster Shorter Catechism. The handout uses the Heidelberg Catechism to give additional insights. Ask the questions and let the women read the answers.
   - Encourage the women to think intentionally in each petition: How is God glorified and how is His kingdom extended as we make this petition.

7. "Our Father in heaven." Handout question 3

   - John Calvin:

> In calling God "Father," we put forward the name "Christ." With what confidence would anyone address God as "Father"? Who would break forth into such rashness as to claim for himself the honor of a son of God unless we had been adopted as children of grace in Christ? . . . By the great sweetness of this name he frees us from all distrust, since no greater feeling of love can be found elsewhere than in the Father. Therefore he could not attest his own boundless love toward us with any surer proof than the fact that we are called "children of God" (1 John 3:1). . . . *Our* Father: From this fact we are warned how great a feeling of brotherly love ought to be among us, since by the same right of mercy and free liberality we are equally children of such a father.[3]

3. John Calvin, *Institutes of the Christian Religion* (Philadelphia: The Westminster Press), 899, 901.

- Martyn Lloyd-Jones:

Just stop for a moment and remind yourself of what you are about to do. We can put it in a phrase. Do you know that the essence of true prayer is found in the two words in verse 9, "Our Father"? I suggest that if you can say from your heart, whatever your condition, "My Father," in a sense your prayer is already answered. It is just this realization of our relationship to God that we so sadly lack. . . . God in His almightiness is looking at you with a holy love and knows your every need. . . . He is much more anxious to bless you than you are to be blessed.[4]

- You may want to ask volunteers to read John 20:17; Romans 8:15; 1 John 3:1.

8. "Hallowed be your name." Handout question 4

    - A.W. Pink:

Our primary duty in prayer is to disregard ourselves and to give God the preeminence in our thoughts, desires, and supplications. This petition necessarily comes first, for the glorifying of God's great name is the ultimate end of all things.[5]

- The contrast here is between God's glory and our own glory. This is the ultimate contrast between the true woman and the new woman.
- We honor or dishonor His name by our thoughts, words, and actions. There is so much to dull and

4. D. Martyn Lloyd-Jones, *Studies in the Sermon on the Mount* (Grand Rapids: Wm. B. Eerdmans Publishing), 52, 56.

5. Arthur W. Pink, *The Beatitudes and the Lord's Prayer* (Grand Rapids: Baker Books, 1979), 83.

desensitize us to the holiness of God. We begin to take Him and His name casually. Learn to whisper this prayer each time we hear His name defamed.

9. "Your kingdom come." Handout question 5
   - The contrast here is between my kingdom and God's kingdom. The issue is authority. Do I live under my rule or do I submit to God's rule and pray for His kingdom to come in each situation?

10. "Your will be done, on earth as it is in heaven." Handout question 6
    - Here the issue is governance. The contrast is between my will and God's will.
    - John Calvin:

> We may wish nothing from ourselves but his Spirit may govern our hearts; and while the Spirit is inwardly teaching us we may learn to love the things that please him and to hate those which displease him. In consequence, our wish is that he may render futile and of no account whatever feelings are incompatible with his will.[6]

- In each of these first three petitions, we need to pray from Ephesians 3: Give me power to desire your glory rather than my own, to submit to your authority rather than my own, and to desire your will rather than my own. This is a work of grace that God accomplishes in His children. As this is done in our own hearts, God is glorified and His kingdom is extended.

6. Calvin, *Institutes of the Christian Religion*, 907.

11. The next three petitions focus on our needs. Again, with each petition ask: How is God glorified and His kingdom extended?

12. "Give us this day our daily bread." Handout question 7
    - In the Hebrew, bread is a generic term referring to our physical needs.
    - How does this petition glorify God?

To answer this, ask another question: If we have employment, why should we ask God for food and housing? What does asking Him acknowledge? It acknowledges that He is the owner of it all, and that whatever we have—job, home, clothes—are gifts from Him. We are stewards of those gifts. It acknowledges our dependence on Him.

What does asking engender in us? Humility, gratitude, and responsibility.

This attitude about our possessions glorifies Him and extends His kingdom in our hearts. Also, emphasize that this is an important perspective to teach our children.

13. "And forgive us our debts, as we also have forgiven our debtors." Handout question 8

    - A. W. Pink:

> Forgiveness is not to be demanded as something due us, but requested as a mercy. . . . This petition implies a felt sense of sin, a penitent acknowledgement thereof, a seeking of God's mercy for Christ's sake, and the realization that He can righteously pardon us. Its presentation should ever be preceded by self-examination and humiliation.[7]

7. Pink, *The Beatitudes and the Lord's Prayer,* 115.

- Martyn Lloyd-Jones:

The man who knows he has been forgiven, only in and through the shed blood of Christ, is a man who must forgive others. He cannot help himself. If we really know Christ as our Saviour our hearts are broken and cannot be hard, and we cannot refuse forgiveness. . . . This petition is full of the atonement, it is full of the grace of God. . . . The thing is absolute and inevitable. True forgiveness breaks a man, and he must forgive. So that when we offer this prayer for forgiveness we test ourselves in that way.[8]

- It glorifies God for us to pray this petition from the heart because it means a life of repentance, faith, and obedience.

14. "And lead us not into temptation, but deliver us from evil." Handout question 9

    - A. W. Pink:

The word *tempt* has a twofold significance in Scripture, though it is not always easy to determine which of the two applies in a particular passage: (1) *to try (the strength of), to put to the test*; and (2) *to entice to do evil*. . . . God often permits Satan to assault and harass us, in order to humble us, to drive us to Himself, and to glorify Himself by manifesting more fully to us His preserving power.[9]

- In John 17 Jesus prayed that God will keep us and sanctify us. Joining Him in this prayer extends His kingdom in our hearts and empowers us to shine His light to push against the kingdom of darkness. As

8. Lloyd-Jones, *Studies in the Sermon on the Mount*, 75–76.
9. Pink, *The Beatitudes and the Lord's Prayer*, 118, 121

we live in the kingdom of darkness, we need to pray continually that we will not become like it.

15. "For yours is the kingdom and the power and the glory, forever. Amen." Handout question 10

    - A. W. Pink:

> "For Thine is the Kingdom." These words set forth God's universal right and authority over all things, by which He disposes of them according to His pleasure. God is Supreme Sovereign in creation, providence, and grace. He reigns over heaven and earth, all creatures and things being under His full control. The words "and the power" allude to God's infinite sufficiency to execute His sovereign right and to perform His will in heaven and earth. Because He is the Almighty, He has the ability to do whatsoever he pleases. He never slumbers nor wearies (Ps. 121:3, 4); nothing is too hard for Him (Matt. 19:26); none can withstand Him (Dan. 4:35). All forces opposed to Him and to the Church's salvation He can and will overthrow. The phrase "and the glory" sets forth His ineffable excellency: since He has absolute sovereignty over all and commensurate power to dispose of all, He is therefore all-glorious. God's *glory* is the grand goal of all His words and ways, and of His glory He is ever jealous (Isa. 48:11, 12). To Him belongs the exclusive glory of being the Answerer of prayer.[10]

    - We begin where we started. What was Jesus' first petition? "Father, the hour has come; glorify your Son that the Son may glorify you" (John 17:1).

16. Handout question 11: Fill in the blank.

10. Ibid., 131.

12

KINGDOM: HANDOUT

Matthew 6:9–13

1. What others have said about the Lord's Prayer:

Martyn Lloyd-Jones:

Prayer is beyond any question the highest activity of the human soul. Man is at his greatest and highest when, upon his knees, he comes face to face with God. . . . It is at the same time the ultimate test of a man's true spiritual condition. . . . Everything we do in the Christian life is easier than prayer. . . . There is a greater need for guidance at this point than at any other. . . . We need to be taught how to pray, and we need to be taught what to pray for. . . . [The Lord's Prayer] is a perfect synopsis of our Lord's instruction on how to pray, and what to pray for.[1]

A. W. Pink:

It is virtually an epitome of the Psalms and a most excellent summary of all prayer. Every clause in it occurs in the Old

1. Lloyd-Jones, *Studies in the Sermon on the Mount*, 45–48.

Testament, denoting that our prayers must be Scriptural if they are to be acceptable.[2]

2. Contrast

    Matthew 6:5–9—The focus is on ________.
    Matthew 6:9–11—The focus is on ________.

3. "Our Father in heaven."

Heidelberg Catechism Q. 120: Why did Christ command us to call God "our Father"?
A. At the very beginning of our prayer Christ wants to kindle in us what is basic to our prayer—the childlike awe and trust that God through Christ has become our Father. Our fathers do not refuse us the things of this life: God our Father will even less refuse to give us what we ask in faith.

Heidelberg Catechism Q. 121: Why the words "in heaven"?
A. These words teach us not to think of God's heavenly majesty as something earthly, and to expect everything for body and soul from his almighty power.

4. "Hallowed be your name."

Heidelberg Catechism Q. 122: What does the first request mean?
A. "Hallowed be your name" means, help us to really know you, to bless, worship, and praise you for all your works and for all that shines forth from them: your almighty power, wisdom, kindness, justice, mercy, and truth. And it means, help us to direct all our living—what we think, say, and do—so that your name will never be blasphemed because of us but always honored and praised.

2. Pink, *The Beatitudes and the Lord's Prayer,* 73.

5. "Your kingdom come."

   Heidelberg Catechism Q. 123: What does the second request mean?
   A. "Your kingdom come" means, rule us by your Word and Spirit in such a way that more and more we submit to you. Keep your church strong, and add to it. Destroy the devil's work, destroy every force which revolts against you and every conspiracy against your Word. Do this until your kingdom is so complete and perfect that in it you are all in all.

6. "Your will be done, on earth as it is in heaven."

   Heidelberg Catechism Q. 124: What does the third request mean?
   A. "Your will be done on earth as it is in heaven" means, help us and all people to reject our own wills and to obey your will without any back talk. Your will alone is good. Help us one and all to carry out the work we are called to, as willingly and faithfully as the angels in heaven.

7. "Give us this day our daily bread."

   Heidelberg Catechism Q. 125: What does the fourth request mean?
   A. "Give us today our daily bread" means, do take care of all our physical needs so that we come to know that you are the only source of everything good, and that neither our work and worry nor your gifts can do us any good without your blessing. And so help us to give up our trust in creatures and to put trust in you alone.

8. "And forgive us our debts, as we also have forgiven our debtors."

Heidelberg Catechism Q. 126: What does the fifth request mean?
A. "Forgive us our debts, as we also have forgiven our debtors" means, because of Christ's blood, do not hold against us, poor sinners that we are, any of the sins we do or the evil that constantly clings to us. Forgive us just as we are fully determined, as evidence of your grace in us, to forgive our neighbors.

9. "And lead us not into temptation, but deliver us from evil."

Heidelberg Catechism Q. 127: What does the sixth request mean?
A. "And lead us not into temptation, but deliver us from the evil one" means, by ourselves we are too weak to hold our own even for a moment. And our sworn enemies—the devil, the world, and our own flesh—never stop attacking us. And so, Lord, uphold us and make us strong with the strength of your Holy Spirit, so that we may not go down to defeat in this spiritual struggle, but may firmly resist our enemies until we finally win the complete victory.

10. "For yours is the kingdom and the power and the glory, forever. Amen."

Heidelberg Catechism Q. 128: What does your conclusion to this prayer mean?
A. "For yours is the kingdom and the power and the glory forever" means, we have made all these requests of you because, as our all-powerful king, you not only want to, but are able to give us all that is good; and because your holy name, and not we ourselves, should receive all the praise, forever.

Heidelberg Catechism Q. 129: What does that little word "Amen" express?
A. "Amen" means, This is sure to be! It is even more sure that God listens to my prayer, than that I really desire what I pray for.

11. How do we call on God in truth? By praying as He ____________ us to pray.

"When we pray aright, we look beyond time and into eternity and measure present things by their connection with the future."[3]

A. W. Pink

3. Pink, *The Beatitudes and the Lord's Prayer,* 133.